MW00937517

auntie

The Healing
Pan American Flight 001

patron of the arts and surrogate Mommy love Richard

Richard Jellerson

outskirts press

The Healing
Pan American Flight 001
All Rights Reserved.
Copyright © 2018 Richard Jellerson
v5.0

The opinions expressed in this manuscript are solely the opinions of the author and do not represent the opinions or thoughts of the publisher. The author has represented and warranted full ownership and/or legal right to publish all the materials in this book.

This book may not be reproduced, transmitted, or stored in whole or in part by any means, including graphic, electronic, or mechanical without the express written consent of the publisher except in the case of brief quotations embodied in critical articles and reviews.

Outskirts Press, Inc.
http://www.outskirtspress.com

ISBN: 978-1-9772-0024-2

Cover Photo by Pat Crist. Cover art by Brenda Buffalin. © 2018 All rights reserved - used with permission.

Outskirts Press and the "OP" logo are trademarks belonging to Outskirts Press, Inc.

PRINTED IN THE UNITED STATES OF AMERICA

Table of Contents

Foreword

I had never heard of Pan American Flight 001 when my cousin Richard told me about it. Chances are, neither have you reading this now. From 1947 to the 70's, a ticket on this luxury airliner took you around the world for a year, visiting San Francisco, Honolulu, Hong Kong, Bangkok, Delhi, Beirut, Istanbul, Frankfurt, London, and New York. You could disembark anywhere along the route and stay if you wanted: two days or two months. The flight came through every couple of days, so you could continue the journey at your whim. Far more than a vacation, this offered adventure. For Richard, it became an odyssey of healing.

I didn't really get to know Richard until well into adulthood. He is ten years my senior and our rare family gatherings meant we were aware of each other but didn't know each other well. Growing up, I knew he had been a helicopter pilot in Vietnam. For those who remember that time in our country, our young men came home, not to parades and gratitude for their service, but distrust, sometimes open hostility. In the Civil War PTSD was called "Soldier's Heart", in WWII, "Shell Shock." All wars leave their nightmares. But our Vietnam vets had to suffer their physical and emotional scars in a country that chose not to care about them.

I never saw any such Veteran issues with Richard. He was always affable, full of humor, and interested in whatever I was doing. I assumed some guys got through the war unscathed. I was well into my fifties before I learned about the harrowing battles and bloodshed that Richard had faced. I learned about it when he told me the story of how he chose to return to America after the war. He took the long way home. He bought a ticket on Pan Am Flight 001.

For the better part of a year he took his time, explored, hung out, ate, drank, had long conversations, found friends, lovers, and joie de vivre. In that time, through the people whose lives he shared, he reunited with humanity.

When he told me the story, I joked that it was *Eat Pray Love* meets *Apocalypse Now*. Richard wasn't unscathed by the war, but he took a chance that a trip around the world might get him ready to go home. He didn't know that he would find healing.

Todd Mattox

Preface

"The Healing" is not a war story. It does address some wartime experiences of mine for context. It is rather a story about the innate kindness and warmth of humanity and the power of human touch. It's about the ability we each have for those who are willing, to reach across to those who are accepting- and heal open wound chasms of pain and loss. This humanity can often be simply shared and offered to another with just a hug, an honest, firm handshake or a squeeze of the shoulder. In its simplest form it might be just a welcome smile from a total stranger.

The healing discussed in this book took me by surprise. At first, I didn't recognize I needed to heal. I expect a reader wouldn't recognize any need either without the insights I've made about my flying combat missions in Vietnam. I was never physically wounded. But the psychic wounds from the inhumanity that is war were deep and open.

More open and much deeper than I knew.

I need to thank some people. Both Pamela Wheeler and Vivian Callahan did read-throughs and made insightful often powerful suggestions. Many of their thoughts were incorporated into the writing. I want to thank Bill Fortier as well for his diligent edit. So appreciate Brenda Buffalin's cover art and the cover photograph years ago by Pat Crist. Special thanks to Shirley Schulz, my beloved Aunt and patron of the arts.

My cousin, Todd Mattox however deserves some very special thanks. A successful, accomplished screenwriter himself it was over a good single-malt scotch that he, not I, came up with the idea that this journey of mine was a book. He then acted as muse, editor, occasional rewriter; slave-driver and often interrogator leading me to relive the experience. And we grew even closer through the process. Writing about it was like taking a healthy healing journey once again. So, thank you Cousin Todd.

Introduction

Didn't want to go home yet. Kinda surprised myself. It was 1970.

After being an Army helicopter pilot in Vietnam I was sure I'd just want to get back to family and friends, backyard barbeques, and Southern California beaches. With living in Hawaii for nearly a year, a year-long Army flight school and two tours in Vietnam I'd been away from home three and a half years. So why didn't I want to go straight home? I was out of the Army, once again a civilian. So why?

Didn't yet recognize I needed healing. Just felt a restlessness and wanderlust I thought I could address by traveling the world. Wanted to get to know other people, visit other cultures and explore this planet. So, instead of going straight back to Los Angeles, family and home after my second tour, I bought a ticket on Pan American Flight One. This was an amazing concept from the company who pioneered passenger aviation. The ticket was a magic carpet to many countries around the planet.

Between my two tours of duty in Vietnam I was given a month leave. I took the long way back to the states: Pan American Flight One. The Army bought that first airline ticket for me. Part of the deal for my agreeing to a second tour. The flight stopped at most of the world's major cities. That first time though, I had to make the entire trip around the world in one month. The best part and a truly unique innovation though, was that the ticket was good for an entire year! It allowed you to get off and stay in a country as long as you wanted. Then get back on the next Pan Am Flight One headed west. Spent three weeks of that first trip in England and a couple other wonderful places. The hound had been blooded though. There was more going on in me then than I understood. I wanted to see this planet.

Calcutta, Istanbul, Tehran, Bangkok, Hong Kong, Berlin, London... the world. Spin the schoolroom globe. I went alone.

A year and a half earlier, mid-December 1969 Long Binh, Vietnam. It's at least a hundred degrees, likely more. Directly under the focal point of the sun a large amphitheater boils over with thousands of soldiers waiting for the Bob Hope USO Christmas Show to begin.

Sweat. Incurable thirst. Dust. Mind-sucking heat, mind-sucking war. Only takes a year of your young life if you survive it. Then years of hesitation to admit you had a part in it. I think, very much like being in denial of a drug or alcohol addiction, this only postpones the cure. The healing.

The daily rhythm of this war lies between the poetry and power chords of rock and roll, the guttural cadence of a Huey helicopter, and your own cherished heartbeat. These pagan and visceral poundings are gone on this special day with Bob Hope. They're strangely replaced with swing music and punch lines. Les Brown and His Band of Renown plays, *"Thanks for the Memories."* Then Bob is on stage with his golf club making jokes.

No, Mr. Hope, it doesn't seem like Christmas with the heat and the smell. Sides don't ache from laughter. Eyes don't seem to fill with joyous tears. The laughter seems somehow strained or caused by something other than humor. But we all know Mr. Hope doesn't have to be here. He hasn't spent a Christmas at home since before most of us were born. And what he's saying is funny. We're just out of practice.

It's probably been months since any of us really laughed at anything. The applause is heavy. We're entertained. Grateful. Mr. Hope is a hero in his own right.

Then with a wave of his putter...there's silence. Bob says, "Here's what you came to see…Let's bring out the girls!" They're what we came to see all right. And before they hit the stage a thousand soldiers detonate into applause, catcalls, hoots and whistles. A thousand man-boys who haven't seen an American woman in months and months erupt as one.

In our fleeting youth we had always taken the presence of women for granted. We stand and yell, "Bring them on!" We all think at first, being young boys, just for our entertainment. Our pleasure. Our inspection.

Then suddenly, they're on stage. And they are more beautiful than anyone of us here remembers. They are more graceful, feminine and wondrously curved than our tormented night dreams or carefully thought out daydreams remind us.

They are met with silence. Our noise stopped as quickly as it started. The last irreverent catcall died stifled on a startled G.I.'s tongue. The band plays. The girls smile. Without thinking, like returning a yawn, we smile back. Some of us stare, awed by the reality that there is such a thing as Woman.

We're all brave, scared boys on a forced march to become men. For months, the guys in the infantry have lived with blister-hot steel guns and tanks all day. Then slept fitfully on the same angry metal all night as it cools. Hot and muggy all day here. Warm and muggy all night.

Anyone who has seen action here for more than a month is tougher and older inside. We've worked cynicism into an art form. We are a hard bunch to surprise or impress. Yet we all stand off-balance, open-mouthed. The void left by the absence of women in our lives is a fresh and painful realization. And another surprise we're not prepared for. We need them. And maybe not just sexually as we constantly imagine. We live under fire there too, assaulted and oppressed.

Maybe the need is a balancing force, a nurturing partnership. The first glimmering recognition of a grand design and higher purpose to both life and this amazing man-woman thing seeps into our hormone deluged brains. It's taken their sudden loss and surrogate reappearance months later to teach us something new again. Maybe it isn't just about how they fit in their jeans. Maybe it's how we fit into each other's lives.

With this realization, living through even just one more day in this place becomes desperately more important. Here are new reasons to survive.

As the girls dance I can see resolve hardening some eyes and expressions. Most of us in this war haven't lived long enough yet to clearly view the big picture. I'm twenty years old flying Army helicopters in combat. The average American soldier in this war is a teenager. Hell, my first crew chief was seventeen. Idiot lied about his age to get over here.

All of us had been dropped into an emotional tempest. But by nature of our upbringing in America, the only acceptable outlet for emotions here is anger. Other emotions – hell, all the rest are held in check. We couldn't let them out of the maze even if we knew the way. Be brave. Don't look elsewhere for strength. Be a rock! A soldier! A man! We try. We internalize everything. Some of us apparently can't do that. Those guys go nuts and get sent home early.

It already feels like childhood was just a dream I had once. I think the dream weakened, began slipping away and ended in a sultry mist the same dull grey, overcast morning we flew into Fire Support Base Diamond. Fire support bases were small outposts built to protect sections of the countryside with villages or bridges nearby. They were armed with artillery, Howitzers, and often Special Forces and reconnaissance units.

Widely used during the Vietnam War, their purpose was to provide artillery fire support to infantry operating in areas beyond the normal range of support from their own base camps. FSBs follow several plans, their shape and construction varied based on the terrain they occupied. Often, like FSB Diamond, they were star shaped allowing for defensive crossfire.

They were called, "Human Wall" charges. All night long, hundreds and hundreds of massed enemy forces coming all at once had attacked the little base carved out of a dense jungle. This meant even the base's big cannons were fired zero elevation–at ground level–directly at the charging enemy. As we flew in that morning there were four hundred dead Viet Cong bodies and body parts flung in a horrific surreal display, some still hanging in the perimeter wires.

Growing up here is ugly, brutal and fast. We handle it as best we can.

But at what cost? Only time will tell I think.

There is deep frustration with the prosecution of this war. We airlift our infantry hopscotching in and out of LZs chasing the enemy to the borders of either Cambodia or Laos. There the enemy forces cross the border and immediately turn around and thumb their noses at us. Getting permission to fire back at the enemy in a "No Fire" zone was senseless.

Oddly, another paradox was "Targets of Opportunity" No permission needed for these. There were only two: Sampans on waterways at night. Civilians wouldn't be out after dark. Had to be enemy activity.

The other targets of opportunity were elephants. The enemy used elephants for transporting heavy guns and stores. Amazing how we could have little to no remorse firing at the Viet Cong. And the same gunship crew couldn't bring themselves to kill those beasts.

At the end of some days in the 116th Combat Assault Helicopter Company's shabby officer's club fights would often break out between platoons. Mostly just distractions to relieve the tension, they weren't real fights. They were just pushing and shoving each other around the rattan furniture. And there were rules. Clean fights, everyone ended up drunk and laughing in our mud hole "pool." Anybody who got carried away or got angry and fought dirty though, would find themselves in the slit trench behind the latrines. Nasty.

In battle we are stoic and brave largely because of peer pressure. None of us have permission from the rest to admit we are scared. Very soon we learn there's no time or place for fear here anyway.

There's a weird, esoteric bond forged with others in combat. No one reaches out for strength. Strength is offered in the clandestine agreement that we are brothers in arms. We are in this together, counting on each other. And we trust one another with our lives, whatever the hell comes down that pike.

It was us against them. Naively at first, we all thought *them* should have only been the enemy. But mostly over there it felt like us against everyone.

We couldn't fight Washington DC. We were losing against the American public. When you went home, family and friends questioned what we were doing. You could get a discount on airline tickets for flying through the states with your uniform on when on leave. Most of us would rather not take the ridicule and scorn. So, we paid full price and flew in our civilian clothes- hiding from our own country.

But nobody beat us on our missions: Washington, the folks at home, the press. Nothing came between us when we were under fire. We took care of each other like everyone else there was our little brother. If you have little brothers, you know what I mean. It's a strange code of "You pick on them, you *will* answer to me." Where it's spawned and nurtured I'm not sure, just an instinct. There was no mission we wouldn't take, nothing any of us wouldn't do for the other guys there. Absolutely nothing. Our highest priority in that crazy war wasn't "winning." It was taking care of each other.

No way though do you show your vulnerability or fear here in this macho, testosterone-thick environment. R and R's and leaves are for stocking up on warmth and comfort. Even if you can't tell a woman you're scared, at least you can choke back a whole lot of unsightly fears and ghastly premonitions by holding her in your arms. It's something intricately psychic or maybe just the simple warmth of two people who care for each other...even if for just a moment in time. It doesn't matter. It works. There's nothing quite like it.

But not with these women on the USO stage. They're untouchable.

The effect of these four women on thousands of G.I.'s is disturbing and unsettling. No one looks away even to carry on a conversation with a friend. Some of us, like myself, concentrate on just one girl at a time. We memorize her.

Every form, color, nuance, and texture is committed to memory. Heat, thirst, and fear all drop away as we vicariously slake an older, much deeper thirst.

We embrace old hungers. Dreams of home towns, grassy parks, bare feet, blue jeans, summer nights, drive-in movies, hamburgers and fries, a girl at your side and being safe again at home shine on the faces of many of us. Couple guys actually sat back down and cried. Tears: a vestigial carry over from recent childhood.

Most of us think deep down we're running out of both luck and time to spend griddle-hot and wretched-scared in a country none of us think we're saving anyway.

Being brave is a rite of passage here. But it takes a lot out of you. If it doesn't take your life or limbs, it still seems to extract a heavy measure of your heart or spirit. Nothing in life matters here more than getting back home. Even the slang here for home, *The World,* came from the sheer disbelief in what we see every day in this war. Surely, we must be on another planet. You've got to get back home to get back what you lost. If you can do either.

The girls eventually do their skits. Then Bob is saying that recently men had reached the moon. Our men. "One in particular…The first to set foot…"

Every soldier vaulted to his feet together, applauding loud and hard. It wasn't one at a time, a smattering here and there then everyone else badgered or guilted into it. No, it was one universal thought, one fluid action. Shyly it seemed, Neil Armstrong walked out to center stage. There's no whistling – it's disrespectful, just explosive applause! 110-degree heat. A minute goes by. Mr. Armstrong shuffles self-consciously. A minute and half times a thousand men all standing in incredible heat, applauding relentlessly. No one looks to his fellow soldiers for approval of this ovation outbreak.

No one back in *The World* knows better than these soldiers what courage is all about. It's worn in war like a uniform you never take off. It gets rank. Bravery isn't running out under fire to save a wounded buddy. That's adrenaline and anger.

Courage is a constant thing, a slow thing. It's taking one step at a time through dense jungle knowing an unseen wire could trigger a mine and blow your legs off or kill you at any moment. Bravery empowers you over caution and fear during the slow times at war when you do have time to think.

And thinking about all the ways you could *buy it* here could drive you nuts.

Courage is not flying a helicopter into hostile fire to rescue a downed aircrew or wounded infantry from the enemy. Courage is strapping that aircraft on early in the quiet morning, staring for a moment at the instrument panel and starting it anyway. You know a rescue or a medevac under fire will most likely happen that day. Did yesterday. Still, you go. Every morning you just start your aircraft and fly off.

It takes a certain amount of derring-do just to get through the day here knowing that the cool bottle of Coke served by the smiling Vietnamese kid could have ground glass in it. Or the apparently unopened C-ration can is booby-trapped with a tightly wound band razor. Courage isn't going over the top to assault the enemy lines. There aren't any lines. The bad guys might even be your own Vietnamese scouts. Or your Vietnamese barber with his razor at the back of your neck.

There truly are no safe areas after dark. No safe places for your body or your heart for a solid year. It takes guts just to shut your eyes at night. It takes balls just to be in this country. But it took a big "Brass Set" to be the first man on the moon. That's what three or four minutes of standing ovation in 110-degree heat is all about. An instant icon for thousands of brave young men.

The just now uncomfortable hero tries very hard to hide behind a skinny mike stand. He's not sure he should wave anymore. He looks to Bob Hope for direction. Hope is equally stunned and overwhelmed by this outburst.

We needed to openly salute this man, this warrior. We needed to recognize and applaud his courage far more than we ever needed to laugh.

We're the brave young men during the fear, anger, pain, and noise of battle. But Neil Armstrong, in the silence of space, in the quiet, unpretentious yet absolute confidence in his own skill as a pilot, taught every one of us here what it truly means to be a hero. Neil Armstrong: a hero for thousands of heroes.

The offered brotherhood gets you through the fighting.

The healing you do on your own.

It'll be good someday to get on that Pan American Boeing 707 and out of this country. Going just about anywhere else on the planet. Oversized leather seats, air-conditioned comfort, food and drink service with smiling stewardesses.

Left Vietnam after two tours flying Army helicopters. This meant flying infantry troops into combat with our helicopters in tight formations. Fly into a hot landing zone and drop off those amazing infantry guys under fire. Go back in as a single ship medevac to pick up our wounded, maimed and dead. Then go back into the LZ with the full flight, pick them up and fly them off to another small patch of hell.

Seemed redundant and purposeless. Felt nothing was gained. And everything lost…my youth, the war, perspective…

Death is the enemy. The planned obsolescence of our lives is old age. Like many of us, I've looked the enemy in the eye a couple of times. A dirt bike accident in the California desert. Vietnam. Cancer more recently.

Acceptance removes fear. Gradually, or even easily and quickly sometimes, the idea of our individualized conception of our own death becomes less an abstract. Then oddly, even less a distraction. It's simply a piece of the puzzle, a part of the equation. The inevitable norm. Acceptance however, does not explain sacrifice.

How does any human move his life paradigm to a position of sacrifice? How does a person make and accept that decision willfully against the very imperative of his own prescient being?

At nineteen going on twenty, I could see the enemy below me several hundred feet, straight down the side of a Huey helicopter. I was stationed at Cu Chi, Vietnam with the 116th. We flew combat with the pilot's and cargo doors removed to reduce a little weight. And I think facilitate a quick egress if shot down. Drafty sure, but the view was awesome.

Only a few weeks out of Army flight school I was a co-pilot on my second or third day flying a combat assault. Army helicopter crews flew troop insertions, extractions and medevacs all day, every day. The same missions for up to a full year if you made it. A lot of us didn't.

At the Army Aviation Museum at Fort Rucker, Alabama where we all trained, there are 4,374 names chiseled into a small, elegant, wall. These are the Army aircrew members we lost there, crew-chiefs, door gunners, and pilots. I knew a lot of them. Three of them were friends of mine. We flew together. Their names now on a simple, solemn gold wall. And still at the edge of my consciousness daily. Mike Goeller. Charlie Danielson. Fred Follette.

The enemy below this day was a wonder to see. They ran at full speed through the jungle in those light brown uniforms and pith helmets carrying all their weapons. These North Vietnamese Army Regulars were fully committed to get to our landing zone ahead of us. They ran through the humid, deep green, overheated jungle with only one thought: shoot down the helicopters.

At one level I understood their goal this day was to kill me. Still, this was the first time I had ever seen them. I hadn't yet seen them shooting at my friends or myself. I had been taught that they were my enemy. My country's enemy. Until then I had only intellectually embraced even the concept of enemy.

Moments later, at a visceral level, with primal understanding and an irrevocable acceptance, they became my enemy. This life-changing perception came with the amazing muzzle velocity of a bullet. I was close enough to see the obsidian eyes of the black pajama clad Viet Cong soldier just now popping up from behind a dry rice paddy dike, shooting right at me. Me! He didn't even know me, but hate filled his heart. I saw it in his eyes. Holding that machine gun, with all his being he wanted to kill me. Heavy with troops and on short final only feet from my touchdown point, there were no evasive measures to be taken with my aircraft. He wanted me to die. I wanted to live.

The Pledge of Allegiance, life, liberty and the pursuit of happiness instantly meant nothing. Death was my enemy.

My door gunner with his heavy M-60 mounted machine gun and the

infantry on board were all shooting back at the young soldier. A fusil-
lade of heavy, hot lead rounds poured out of the cargo bay. Everyone
on board was shooting back at him so that he, rather than I, would die
that day. He, or she, actually disappeared under the torrent of heavy
return fire. I was fine with that. Still am forty some years later.

Them or me; death is the enemy. I'll never know who they left behind.

But I lived through that day and many more like it.

Typical tough life decisions are those such as career choice or whom
you will marry. Kill or be killed is one of the easiest decisions any human ever makes.

Fighting for one's life at the expense of, indeed the sacrifice of one's
own life is well documented. Historically men have fought through
the ages for freedom and liberty, resources, family, land, conjured
up borders and esoteric ideals. These wars initiated by so few end
in death for many. During the 1850s England's armies were always
somewhere fighting what Rudyard Kipling would term "The savage
wars of peace." Over a century and a half later these savage wars of
peace continue.

I've been told that what we did in Vietnam was heroic. No. We did
what was expected after training and the bonds formed under fire.
There were so many innocents destroyed by that war. On both sides.
Looking back, I see it now.

The will to live, the determination that another won't take one's life
away is an innate mandate. This imperative worth fighting and killing
for exists throughout nature. Animals and plants alike know this fight.
Each of us has an overriding contract implied with our own being:
Live. Yet, there's a pattern here. Youth at the apex of their power and

with life full in front of them yet sacrificing their lives is not purely a middle-eastern or religious phenomenon.

In 1993, nineteen Army Rangers died in Mogadishu for a credo: "Never leave anyone behind!" Wounded or dead, you bring them home with you. These young men all died for the body of an Army helicopter pilot trapped in his downed aircraft. He was probably dead before the young Rangers ever even moved toward his hostile position. And likely, they knew it.

September 11th, 2001: the other American "Day That Will Live in Infamy." If you are old enough you realize that old saying, "The good old days..." now has a specific before and after date. Along with 2,667 innocents in the towers and 156 innocents on the planes, 317 firemen lost their lives. The firemen, amazingly, were already prepared to die if they must. As part of their value system, their credo, they were ready to sacrifice their lives to save others. And they did. They were running into both buildings as others were trying to run out.

To truly embrace as your option, not just a catchy slogan or a bumper sticker: "Your life is worth more than mine" is an incredibly noble commitment but not logical. If life is the imperative, willfully giving it up is an anomaly. It's baldly and acutely an aberration.

Firemen and policemen wake up every morning to the fatalistic acceptance that it could happen. They could die that day. Fire is one enemy, deadly criminals another. Both groups train hard to have their people see survival at shift's end. But, if irrevocably demanded, they will sacrifice themselves for the rest of us.

Young Army Rangers, Special Forces and many other elite military groups are taught that if you are a chosen member of their special team you proudly accept the credo of sacrifice. Indeed, all military branches work hard to weed out those who can't accept the possibility that they may be asked to die for their brethren.

Actually, they don't "put it in you." They don't "make you," as the ads suggest, "Army Strong." They find those who have it in them. Then all branches of militaries around the world cultivate and nurture that spirit relentlessly into dedication and monastic conviction.

There are differences between states of acceptance or willingness to give up one's life. Yet the mechanisms that enable a human to accept this as a possible, probable or even a desirable outcome are inevitability similar. Caught up in a higher cause like a war, right or wrong, people around you count on you, need you. This drive overcomes all fears and compels you to take any action required.

You must go to a very dark place in your heart to get through the days and nights of combat. Once out of combat that dark place stays with you. Sometimes forever.

Then one day, it was just all over. Military obligation fulfilled. Hard time served. At the end of my second tour in country horrific images would be seared into my consciousness forever. But it was over. I could go home now, remarkably unharmed physically.

I was within three days of starting home and getting out of the Army. I was still in Saigon at our bar built next to the villa that housed both Four Star General's flight crews and our gunship escort crews. I was only waiting for my paperwork. There I was recruited by both Air America and the Navy. The Navy wanted to transition me into jets, so they would have high-time dual rated pilots; rotary and fixed wing. I told the guy in the snappy Navy uniform, "No." Never regretted that decision until the movie, "Top Gun" came out in the eighties. Air America was the CIA's air force flying clandestine missions mostly in Laos and Cambodia over the Ho Chi Minh trail. Still don't regret telling them no.

My ship in the 116th was shot up a lot but never shot down. Ask any pilot. A huge difference. Lost a lot of friends. Needlessly it turns out. A lot of good men lost their lives there. Didn't give their lives for their country, lost them. There is a difference. Ask someone in our military.

Left that country still young, but discouraged about human nature. Troubled over my purpose and role on this planet. Felt uncomfortable, disorganized and yes, tricked. Didn't feel like I was ready to go back to America. My country was deeply troubled and divided then. Protests...some violent. So why go back to another war zone?

The offered brotherhood gets you through the fighting.

The healing you do on your own.

Thailand…

THE FIRST LEG of Pan American Flight One took me to Thailand. This very old country looked like most of Vietnam from the air of course. It had intense, lurid green jungles, forested mountains and a huge system of tributaries and rivers. They all lead to the birth mother of all the early civilizations in Southeast Asia, the great Mekong River.

On a hot humid day, I was sitting in the shade at a small dirt strip airport outside Bangkok. This wasn't their municipal or international airport. A small, quiet breeze eased through periodically trying to cool the afternoon. It pushed through a cloying sweet smell of flowers. Were they seen rather than smelled, I imagined they would be purple. Such is the mental assessment of my mind trying to understand an undefined plant odor.

I was waiting for a small feeder line airplane and secretly hoping it would be a twin-engine aircraft. Lots of jungle to fly over trying to get out to a rural village. I was going to another dirt strip somewhere off into another part of Thailand. I would see this country first. My travels then, my journey, would take me to so many places both geographically and psychologically. I was to take many side-trips on this journey. I was exploring the world. And eventually I would learn, exploring myself.

The Thai are a beautiful, gracious people. Most live and work in the cities. Many live in beautiful homes built of pure teak on the many rivers that crisscross their country. These fortunate people go to work, school and the markets by boat. It looks to me a splendid life with tight families living off the land and fresh fish they catch right off their front porch.

THE HEALING

At this small airport I met a Thai girl, maybe in her teens. She was pushing a bright white wooden cart selling soft drinks and headed directly for me. Her beautiful, natural smile became her introduction as a merchant. After selling me a warm Coke she sat on the bench next to me and offered to share her small lunch if we could just talk about America for a while.

Felt to me a strange and uncomfortable request. It surprised me. And I wasn't ready to talk about it. I didn't want to. Had to think about it. I had changed so much that I didn't yet understand my feelings about America. A feeling that often bubbled to the top though, was that I had been betrayed.

Growing up in Southern California was a rich, textured childhood of friends and fun. Don't remember a contentious or otherwise uncomfortable day at school or anywhere else in my life prior to leaving for the military: life on cruise control. Made good money at some part time jobs in Pasadena. I had a beautiful white 57 Chevy coupe to cruise Colorado Boulevard and a couple dirt bikes. Between the beach, beautiful girls, the Mojave Desert with no speed limits, sandlot football and friends, life was full and fun.

I was happy, content, fulfilled. Hadn't yet given thought to what I would do with my life. But didn't feel rushed to figure it out either. It would come to me.

Graduated Pasadena High School and went directly to Pasadena City College for a while. I did get my Associate Degree eventually, but it wasn't easy. So many distractions. Blonde, brunette and redhead distractions were everywhere. Social life and my dance card were full. I went Grunion hunting at night with my friends on the beaches of Southern California. Cruised those same beaches next day looking for young women in bikinis. Went off-road on every trail or road in the vast Mojave Desert behind the mountain range that forms the Los Angeles basin.

Young and healthy I had known some of my good friends all my life up to that point. Assumed then we would all be lifelong friends. Always in touch, always knowing we were there for each other. That *was* my always.

Graduation Pasadena High School 1965

Didn't think I needed to see anything outside California. Didn't need to meet new people, explore new lands, or leave the sublime mystique of Southern California.

Then the war. Life took a hairpin turn on what I thought was going to be a straight stretch of smooth highway ahead.

Waiting for my plane with that sweet Thai girl, I was captivated, enchanted by the candor and honesty of her questions. Those big brown eyes didn't hurt at all either.

In the shelf under the commercial part of the cart holding her entire retail inventory of seven to eight lukewarm sodas she pulled out a sandwich wrap of Thai seafood. Capitalism is flawed but amazing. Probably, if the cokes were even real, she bought them for 50 cents, and sold them for two dollars.

She split her meager lunch in two with her small brown hands and shared it with me. Upbeat and positive she was sure she would go to America someday. Wanted to anyway. Wanted to attend one of our colleges. "What's it really like?" she wanted to know. "Are there really sprawling open parks of grass, free schools, and skyscrapers and …?" On and on she went. Questions tumbled out of her like a bubbling brook after a spring rain.

Eventually I came to realize I could answer her questions and address her curiosity only when she took a breath, should she elect to ever do so. My plane was late, and we spoke for quite a while. She in broken English, me in "pidgin" English along with some sign language. But it worked.

I was trying to remember what America was like. The scenes coming to my mind were like watching old black and white television with periodic crackling, static-laden losses of signal.

Movies and television had fictional illustrations of how life worked in our culture. Inane TV programs with likable families worked their way through issues that always ended well in less than a half-hour. Westerns portrayed gunfights. A cowboy on a barn roof would get shot, grab his stomach, say, "Oh, you got me!" and fall behind the barn. Never saw a wound. But in reality, bullets blow big, raggedy jagged holes in people. And there's blood everywhere.

I wasn't quite sure how I felt about America just yet. I was entertaining thoughts of not going back at all. I was considering immigrating to somewhere else. First thought was Australia but maybe now; Thailand?

I'm sure now that I was then brittle, perhaps broken inside, burnt out emotionally. But somehow this gentle girl was tapping into me. Unknowingly she had revealed a piece of the dichotomy I felt about going home but didn't yet understand. America wasn't what she thought it was anyway. Was it? It certainly wasn't what I thought it had been. My country and I had both changed so much I wasn't sure we would recognize each other.

Didn't know if the American dream was still there at all. My perceptions were clouded, muddled, and had obviously not withstood the chaos of war. My view of life in America had shifted and changed. I had been through an awful lot considering there were no visible scars.

Wasn't at all proud of what I'd seen in America on my thirty-day leave between tours in Vietnam. Seemed freedom of speech had turned into rather an ugly aggression. Opposing sides didn't seem to want to reconcile, just argue. Peaceful demonstrations often turned into riots.

Neither side moved their beliefs forward. Simply moved further and further toward hating and misunderstanding each other. Wasn't reconciled with what I'd seen during either of my tours either. The basest instincts of Man are the daily palette on the canvas of war.

Would I ever understand and embrace the changes in me and my country? The question seemed to loom over an ominous cliff. There would need be a reckoning if my life were to move on. And until I had answers there would be no healing. At least, it seemed that was the order of things. Later I would understand this was not the way of things. Didn't yet know that I needed to heal before questions were answered or my life could move forward.

My jagged, war torn psyche was somehow calmed and quieted by hearing a foreigner speak so lovingly about my homeland. Didn't yet know why her conversation stilled and soothed my senses, why it moved me the way it did. Didn't know the journey I had yet to take. Didn't yet recognize I was even on a journey other than the one for which I had purchased an airline ticket.

Remaining stoic, appearing brave, internalizing everything you see and witness in combat may not be good for you. But there are no choices. So, you play the hand you're dealt. And this morass of suspicions, doubts, fears while witnessing the atrocity of war just continues to fester deep inside you.

If you're having the same nightmare every night and all day again and again, it's not a nightmare.

Certainly, there was no one to come home to who asks, "How was your day, dear?" No counsel but a warm, flat beer at our shabby little officer's club if you didn't have a mission to fly that night.

The young Thai woman and myself talked easily until my plane finally arrived. I don't think I ever knew her name. Didn't realize that hers were only the first warm hands to be outstretched to me trying to bring me back to being human again. There would be more as I traveled around the world leaving war behind.

Several hours later, the single engine Cessna taxi service dropped me further into the Thai outback. I picked up a truck and guide at the small grass airstrip. We took off on a dirt road through the jungle and came across a village. I had the sense the village had prospered happily in its own quiet way for centuries on that very riverbank. It had an open school, one classroom. There were no sides to the one-story building, but it had a metal roof. The only metal roof in the village.

Ten or so children around maybe nine years old to early teens were sitting on wooden benches. I wondered what they were learning? There was a chalkboard with math equations on it. But what else would they need to survive out here? Fishing and hunting skills, if they stay. Language and social skills if they move to an urban environment and plan to have a career in some "civilized" discipline.

Wonder what I could teach them? Wasn't asked to offer any insights anyway.

Just felt I had learned so much I should share. Share what, the horror of war? Humanity chewing away, gnawing like cannibals at each other's bones? I'd rather these children didn't know that, never knew that.

I couldn't have been the first Caucasian they had ever seen. But they stared at me anyway. I know now I was on my way back, taking a complicated, troubled journey back to the human race. The journey I had just finished in war was complicated and troubled too. But now, with the unsolicited help of strangers, I had to find my way back home. Back to me, back to myself who had somehow been left behind. Hopefully, I was still out there, anxiously awaiting my own return.

Couldn't know what the children saw when they looked at me through their sweet, kind, untroubled eyes. Maybe they saw my aura if you will. Had to be one of immersion in death, despair, loss. I was never sure if there were any visible manifestation of my inner disquiet. Perhaps people everywhere just pick up vibrations off troubled fellow beings. All the children looked so happy, clean and healthy. Their youth reminded me of mine so very long ago. Could I have ever been that young?

Hong Kong ...

IN A HUGE, sparkling clean theater near the harbor I sat surrounded by Chinese families and watched "Airport" with Chinese subtitles. I'm the foreigner here. I'm the minority. I'm alone in another peoples' land. They do not share their fears, secrets, biases, and bigotries with me.

Still war-torn I sit, quietly suspecting them of disliking me purely because of my race. What a concept. Judged, cataloged and categorized by skin color. They should be better than that, right? Actually, they probably hadn't given me a thought. I was conjuring up insecurities.

Still, as the families passed by after the film's end, many offered a smile. Only a courtesy perhaps. But maybe a message too, a welcome? Maybe only tolerance. My unrest and discomfort, I believe now, was that I was still in an Asian country. Perhaps after combat with the Vietnamese, I would always resent Asians. I didn't want that. Candidly, I would not, could not accept that. I was not raised to be a bigot or racist.

This was an uncomfortable new feeling in me, a disquiet I recognized in that theatre. Raised by a single mom, a powerful warrior herself, she taught her kids that we were no better than and no less than anyone else. She taught her children a lot more than self-worth. Told us, "Whatever you want, want to be, want from life-go get it! I can't give it to you and neither will anyone else."

Toward the end of her life, as her oldest she confided in me, "I wished I could have given you more, done more for you boys." My brothers and I had lost our only sister in a car crash years ago. Nearly lost mom in the same accident. My reply: "What you gave us is that we are healthy, happy and accept that we work, we play, we understand life. It doesn't get any better than that, mom. You did good."

Poorly said perhaps, but I'm forever grateful I had the chance to tell her that.

Didn't happen quickly, but I consciously decided to get past this stumbling block to a life well-lived. I willed myself to work my way through it. With mom's advice and a strong will I would never be a racist. Many years after this journey I had confirmation that I was over it when I became seriously involved with a beautiful Japanese woman. My dad had issues with her at first, as he was a World War Two veteran. Shortly after he met her and got to know her though, he worked his way through it. Rather quickly I thought. Proud of him.

I witnessed the grand opening of the first McDonald's in Hong Kong. Cabbies and hotel staff told me they couldn't get the franchise open for a long time. No one thought it would work. Day it opened, Chinese families lined around all four sides of a big city block. Good or bad, the planet was homogenizing.

My westward movement around the globe was away from the void of logic, the crucible of pain and self-doubt that is war. Didn't yet know how much I needed to move toward being embraced again by humanity. Didn't know how far I had strayed from it.

My tribe had left me to discover life ballistically. Not real life: War. Not how life on this planet should exist. Growing up in America did not prepare me for who I needed to be to get through Vietnam. Had I been raised in a climate of hate and fear, I'm certain I'd have been better prepared for combat. If I had grown up in a country in constant state of assault by outside aggressors, neighboring countries mostly, I would certainly be a different person. If I had always lived in a combat zone, my country at constant war for decades as our enemy had, I would likely be ready, easily accepting, indeed trained for my role in life. And since it had been my life already, there would be no transitioning back to the real world. Likely no healing required. But I had grown up in the tranquility and safety of America, blessed beyond reason. Against the measure of other countries worldwide I had been born into the sanctuary of a singular democratic republic.

Many of the young Vietnamese on both sides of their civil war were my age. They had been born into, grown up with and lived through war their entire lives. I had survived it as a dilettante. But what was needed now? What next?

The Star Ferry ride between Hong Kong and Kowloon always made me feel crowded but comfortable and tall. Crowded because we were. Not sure there was a load limit or lifeboats for all of us. Comfortable because I'd always felt at home on the water. Tall because literally I was around eight inches taller than everyone else on the boat. I was young and that seemed important.

Bought an Omega Speedmaster Professional Chronograph watch, a pilot's watch. Beautiful craftsmanship, wearing it still today. But the original metal wristband pulled the hairs on my wrist. So, I went back to the Chinese merchant next day. He happily switched the steel wristband to a cheap rubber one and kept the high-end band. Seemed to be enjoying the transaction with a big smile. It was days later on a flight out of Hong Kong's surreal airport when I figured it out. He had taught me a valuable business lesson... Early signs of how the world really works.

Lebanon...

ON PAN AM Flight One, as I remember except for first class, seats weren't assigned. I like window seats. Pilots are control freaks and even as a passenger I must feed my need for situational awareness. Leaving for Lebanon I pushed my overnighter into the overhead and looked out the port at the hustle of an airport's operations. Other passengers are boarding up the steps.

All of us should be a little excited about air travel to a place we've never been. Some passengers though seem jaded to the whole process of beginning a journey. For them maybe the journey wasn't new, just a job. Coming up the aisle there are well-dressed, well-groomed businessmen in nice suits with turbans on their heads. Right behind them there's another guy coming up the aisle but, unlike the rest, kind of scruffy. Unshaven, unkempt, blue jeans, tee shirt, hunting vest, couple cameras slung over his left shoulder. He stops at my row.

"Seat taken? You're American right? Hi, I'm Neal."

There are only two luxurious, wide leather seats in a row. He jams his camera case in the overhead and drops into the aisle seat.

"Hi, Neal." That awkward turning to your side to shake hands is quickly over with.

"Nice to meet you. Where you going? Looks like you're just out of Vietnam."

"Yeah, taking the long way home. How can you tell?"

"The haircut is a dead giveaway, Army. And nobody wears those shirts anymore. And the look."

"The look?" I asked.

"The troubled, thousand-yard stare like, 'What's out there ahead of me?'"

"Great, can't hide."

"Not from me anyway."

"What do you do?"

"I'm a photojournalist, war correspondent. A stringer."

I'm sure he saw a question forming on my face, so he continued.

"Means freelance. I have to find the story, document it and sell it.

Post, LA Times, Time magazine once. Did get my byline out on a few stories about your war."

"Not my war anymore. I'm done. Out. What are you looking for?"

"In my line of work, you always need another conflict. Good to be first to get it, too."

We were loaded up. The ground crew wheeled the steps away from the plane. The stewardess closed the main door. Another was already taking drink orders and offering reading material; magazines. It's 1971. In-flight movies wouldn't be invented for years to come. And would I like steak or fish for dinner tonight?

I asked Neal, "So you go around looking for wars?"

"Yep. You're headed out of a war, and I'm trying to find the next one."

"And where is the next one?"

"I think we're headed right into it. This part of the world has always been ripe for conflicts. Think there's another one brewing up ahead in Lebanon...or nearby." My new traveling companion cleared his throat as if making a presentation to his editor or a client, "See, the Jordanian government recently expelled the Palestine Liberation Organization. In no small measure this was done to end Israel's excuse for continuously raiding into and invading Jordan to fight the PLO. Even though Syria sent troops to aid the PLO, they were forced to move to Lebanon. At the least I'm expecting civil unrest, maybe even protests. Its how these things start."

"Always?"

"Rare when conflicts start with a declaration of war. Usually lots of accusing, screaming and finger pointing before any shots are fired."

"Great, war-starting has a formula. You know, someone said the definition of insanity is doing the same thing over and over but expecting different results. You'd think with war we would know better."

Neal is quiet for a bit. Then from a deep well of cynicism he says, "Can't get around human nature. We've been taking what we want or need from our neighbors since the Stone Age."

"And is that human nature or learned behavior? We should be better than that."

Neal again goes quiet for a moment, fails to answer my question but says, "Hope you find what you need after this. Seen a lot of you guys all lost with thousand-yard stares, trying to figure life out after fighting...Hell, life is fighting."

"Can't buy that." My beer arrived. I had yet to discover the grace and majesty of single malt scotch. "I think you might be even more cynical than I am."

"Probably am." Neal's drink arrived, "Been at it longer too. You're new at it. What are you, twenty years old? I've got about ten years on you."

The plane is being pushed back from the gate. The engines are spooling up one at a time. I ventured, "Do you remember?"

"Remember what? The change?"

I paused a moment, thinking. Was I asking him or myself? "Yeah, how'd you get so cynical, so negative about this life, our world?"

"I don't remember a day or certain incident when I changed or even that I had changed. Until I saw it in everyone around me. Seen it in all the kids they send to war. Like watching a match flare. Righteousness. Patriotism. All hot flame until you see how it is in the world. Then just blackened ash and smoke. Once it flares and gone to ash you can't relight it."

Pessimistic about the world...life itself. Like a lot of people sitting next to each other on planes there are acknowledged times silence is okay, even a good thing. I didn't want to talk to him the rest of the flight. His was not a perspective I wanted to embrace.

But he's persistent, "You know why they prophesied the end of the world; Armageddon- will be here in the Middle East?

I had thought about this before, "I think it's because this region then was the entire known world, the whole universe to any people who then had a language."

"Clever. College?"

"Yeah, and Sunday School. Doesn't matter the where. The dynamic is troubling. Why should there be a great conflict between good and evil? An end at all?"

"No answers. And, ah well, sorry, but I'm kinda tired. Been camping the last few days with an armored division right on the North Vietnamese border. As if they care about borders. I'm going to rest a bit."

Wonder if he's right about the match not re-lighting? Hasn't for him obviously. But what about me? Am I as far-gone as he is? I know I'm not who I was but I'm too young to be a burnt-out hulk, down on life, negative about everything for the rest of my days. On final approach to the Beirut airport I watched the gorgeous, shallowing Mediterranean pass beneath. I thought this next country would be a wonderful place to explore, so much history... couldn't wait to see it. After landing and taxiing to the terminal I had a complete change of heart. Didn't even get off the plane. Sat in air-conditioned comfort and watched, horrified.

"Neal, wake up. I think you found your war."

Outside, racing through waves of heat undulating off the tarmac there were Jeeps with mounted machine guns and armed soldiers. Everything I wanted to leave behind. Fear, tension, intimidation, unrest. I couldn't know then this country would foment and sponsor terrorism. But certainly, this early trouble should have indicated a propensity for disruption and disquiet.

THE HEALING

Grabbing his bag, Neal turns to head down the aisle. "Nice to meet you. Maybe we'll meet again, maybe not. But either way good luck to you."

Shaking hands again, "Good luck to you too. No offense but I hope you're wrong about a war here and that life is just fighting."

He gave me the saddest smile I've ever seen and walked off the plane.

Still in my seat, plane still waiting on the ground I felt a troubling and growing discomfort. What kept these young soldiers from just blasting away at this very vulnerable aircraft: discipline? Orders? Who gave them orders? And the other side of the tension I felt, the angst in my heart was a learned vulnerability. If it all went to hell here, I couldn't shoot back or fly myself out of this one.

I had been a new pilot in Vietnam in late January 1969. By Easter week I was a combat veteran. I was an Aircraft Commander in god-like charge of a million-dollar aircraft, as well as the lives of the three other teenagers in my crew.

I thought of Good Friday, 1969. Dawn is the only peaceful time in Vietnam. But at six in the morning it was melting into the subtle violence of 80-degree heat, 90 percent humidity. After three months in this country I still wasn't used to the early heat and mugginess.

I had just finished pre-flighting my helicopter, making sure the battle-scarred Huey was in flying condition when my co-pilot approached with the weather forecast. "Overcast, tops at six-thousand feet, heavy rains and thunderstorms predicted. Sounds familiar, doesn't it?"

"Yeah," I replied. "I've heard that same forecast every day since I got here. I'll sure be glad to see what their dry season is like!" Such is the innocence of inexperience.

My crew chief and door gunner had arrived with the two M-60 machine guns, and a pile of smaller survival weapons. The co-pilot and I were now in our seats going through the pre-flight checklist and preparing to start the ship. My door gunner, Mike Goeller, is an eighteen-year-old from the middle of America. He was also the best shot of any door gunner in the company.

"Where are we going today, sir?" Mike asked.

"We're working the 'Iron Triangle' again."

"Hell!"

"Close enough." I muttered. And then a little louder, "All clear! Coming hot!" I press the trigger that shoots a flame into the big Lycoming turbine. The engine starts to whine, the gauges respond favorably, and eventually the large heavy blades begin to turn. At idling rpm, with all instruments "in the green," I take a moment to reflect. The "Iron Triangle" is an area of Viet Nam between three villages that holds more well-entrenched Viet Cong per square mile than any other single place in the country.

Years of artillery and B-52 strikes have failed to root them out. We always take heavy fire there. Their tunnel system is four stories deep and twenty years old. It's incredible. They have hospitals, munitions, supply storage, mess halls and dormitories – all underground.

We are *Tail-End Charlie* again today, the last ship in the flight of nine to deposit troops into the flooded rice paddies of South Vietnam. Today, we only have our own gunship cover to precede us into the landing zone. The mission of the gunships will again be to soften up the enemy undoubtedly waiting there.

As we climbed to fifteen hundred feet it is a little cooler now. I can see condensation being forced off the tips of the rotor blades of the other ships in formation like pure white scimitars as the blades slice through the damp air. Soon we will have to leave the relative safety of this altitude, which is – they tell us – "Out of accurate small arms range from the ground." The troops on board are loaded down with all their combat gear. I don't envy them walking around down there after we drop them off.

There's the landing zone. We begin our approach. Simultaneously, those first times, my stomach feels warm and my hands tense on the controls. My mind forces my hands to relax because tense makes for poor flying. But I can't stop my palms from sweating. It'll be much worse at the touchdown point where we have to sit for a few seconds like a wallowing elephant and disgorge our troops.

First few missions in Vietnam my stomach would feel as if someone shoved burning steel into it. Sweat rolled into my eyes. My ears would ring from pure unadulterated fear. And that same ominous question, variously phrased, would scream into my head: "What am I doing here? Why me? Did I need adventure so badly? When will this nightmare end?"

And through all of that I came to learn, my mind would function as it never had before. Icy cool, becalmed like the eye of a storm. My reactions and thought processes were heightened to new speeds and capacities. There was an incomparable exhilaration to it. Fear washes through in waves. Yet deeper down, in some instinctual primal area, calculations and reactions are being doled out at the rate of hundreds per second. The operative thought is, *panic will kill you here.*

So, you sweat some. You allow the occasional gush of fear to pass. And simply take charge – always take charge! Marshall all you've learned. Trust your instincts, senses and skills and do what must be done. You're okay now. The troops are out. Go get more troops to reinforce the ones you just dropped. We're not taking any hits. Let's go! Add power. Lift off. Lunge for altitude. Get out of danger. Start breathing again. It's always like that in a hot LZ.

Now on short approach, I pick out the spot where I will put my air-craft down. As I come closer to where I will land, I can see we are taking fire from the tree line on my right. One enemy machine gun is already zeroed in on my landing spot. I try to slow my descent, pulling hard on the collective pitch control. But with a heavy load of American soldiers I can't alter my short final approach or slow my progress much at all.

Looking between my feet on the pedals, I can see bullets slapping into the inundated rice paddy now two or three feet from my Plexiglas chin bubble. The rounds hit so close now, they splash muddy water onto the bubble. I pull harder on the pitch control, now knowing I'm going to float inevitably into the line of fire. The blades are coning upward from the strain. I can hear the engine losing rpms from the immense overload. Just as I resign myself to losing my feet or legs on this ugly morning, the firing stops. One of our gunships saw my problem and solved it.

My ship has lost most of its power and we settle not quite to the wet ground careful not to get the skids stuck in the mud. Within five seconds the six American soldiers clear the ship. Now, with no added weight, we take off easily, rising hurriedly to join up with the forma-tion and the lunge for precious altitude.

We fly back to pick up the next party of troops. As I said *Tail end*

THE HEALING

Charlie is the last aircraft out of the landing zone, a very vulnerable position. Also, Tail-end is the ship predetermined to break off formation and make any needed medevacs; picking up wounded. Sometimes a heartbreaking mission.

It isn't that I didn't like helping our wounded. I relished that mission more than any other. I'm just not calloused enough for the job. I can never steel myself to avoid being painfully torn up emotionally when I pick up a freshly wounded soldier, one who has just been unbelievably mutilated by a mine or a booby trap.

It's even worse when the medics run short of morphine. Some of these seventeen, eighteen and nineteen-year-olds, who haven't even really lived yet, just scream themselves into delirium, into unconsciousness. Sometimes, all the way into death.

There isn't an aircraft that can get a man in that kind of pain to a hospital fast enough.

Our mission has been the same all week. Today, Good Friday, will be no different. Airlift the same infantry company into the same sector of the Michelin rubber plantation, known to be festering with Viet Cong. Our blades sever the early morning stillness as we land on the tiny airstrip next to the ugly fire support base.

The base is a roughly circular, well-armed pockmark of dirt and steel surrounded by acres of bare no man's land in the middle of a great, dense, intensely green jungle.

Likely awash in adrenaline six American troops nimbly dance aboard in graceful, well-practiced steps. They seemingly ignore the sixty-pound packs on their backs and the untold weight of weapons and ammo.

I spot their squad leader, Sgt. Sandy Johnson. He is a stocky, brown-haired farm boy of about twenty. He impresses me as the hard-fisted, hard-drinking kind who would just as soon scrap here as Kansas or Texas. While this isn't a bar fight my character analysis seems spot-on when I see written on the back of his helmet, a caricature of the Twenty-third Psalm. "Yea, though I walk through the Valley of the Shadow of Death, I will fear no evil, for I am the meanest son of a bitch in this valley!"

A little bravado never hurt a man as he stepped into the evil face of danger.

The young sergeant gives me the thumbs up sign – all are aboard. We're on our way. Much heavier now, we nurse our underpowered ships slovenly into the air looking a lot like fat young penguins trying desperately to learn to fly. Penguins, you certainly know, can't fly at all. In the intense heat and humidity with these loads, helicopters barely fly. It ain't pretty but eventually we arrive again and re-form in formation at a safer, cooler, fifteen hundred feet above ground level. I begin to ready my crew and the young infantry squad leader.

"Listen up! We'll be landing in the LZ from north to south. The gun ships will be rolling in hot on the left. Recon tells us the tree line on that side is full of nasties. So we'll only have the slicks to give us full suppression on the right."

I can see that the old veteran, Sgt. Johnson, knows that if recon is wrong, we will only have nine M-60 machine guns, the ones on the slicks, to handle the right side of our flight. If we do take heavy fire from the right, and the gun team doesn't pick up the cue fast enough, we're in the really deep shit once again.

Knowing the V.C. will be on the run from the first load of troops we dropped off, I head directly for the new Landing Zone. There will be another tough reception waiting for us at this LZ. This we expect. The value of the helicopter assaults to hopscotch combat troops to trouble spots had been established long ago.

Both sides know how important the helicopter is to this war. Our area commanders use troop-carrying helicopters to herd the enemy like a shepherd uses his sheepdogs. The analogy ends there however, as sheep are rarely heavily armed, brilliant guerrilla fighters.

We are closing in on the landing zone now. I look back at Sgt. Johnson briefing his troops. They all give him a hearty, strong "thumbs up" sign, assuring him they understand and are ready for anything. Liars! I lock my special Combat Assault shoulder harness that prevents me from slumping onto the controls and crashing the bird in the event I get shot. I prepare for our hasty descent.

My cheeks feel hot and red. And I begin to sweat again as I did when first facing a hot landing zone. Eventually the surrealness of the situation or the acceptance of my mortality gave me a sense of, "Oh, what the hell…"

No more sweats. No more hot cheeks.

The LZ appears straight ahead and we begin to drop lower and lower, doing ninety to a hundred knots. We are flying in trail, single file formation. We're only about fifteen feet apart main rotor tip to tail rotor. This is no time for watching gauges! But flying this close allows us to enter and leave the LZ together. These tight formations in the air and in the LZ, also allow the gun team to give us maximum coverage.

In the landing area all nine ships will flare simultaneously, slow their descent and forward airspeed, touch down for four to six seconds, regurgitate the troops, and flee for safety. Sounds simple doesn't it?

There is no better target in the eyes of the enemy than a stationary helicopter. The veteran American soldiers I carry know this too. As we come to an abrupt landing, and a short slide, the troops lunge out of the ship and flatten themselves on the ground. I give it full power and we leap into the relative safety of the sky.

Every ship is off and as soon as I'm in the clear. I call flight lead. "Lead, this is Hornet three-three, Tail-end Charlie, you are off-flight of nine."

"Roger, three-three," Comes the succinct, noticeably relieved reply.

We are two minutes out of the LZ when I hear the garbled, inevitable radio call – the fourth or fifth this week. One of the guys we dropped off only a couple minutes ago is already wounded.

I immediately call gunship lead. "Gun Team Lead, this is Hornet three-three returning to last landing zone for serious wounded. Can you cover both sides? I'll shoot the same approach, but I'll land up at the far end of the LZ. They'll pop yellow smoke."

"Gotcha covered three-three. Keep your head down," he responds.

I think to myself, *no shit*. Going back in alone I know I can make a very fast approach and if all goes well, an equally fast exit. Milliseconds count.

This time my aircraft will be the only target on the LZ.

I line the ship up with the field and nose it over. I take most of the pitch out of the blades and bleed off rpm to avoid a rotor over speed.

THE HEALING

We're pushing a hundred and ten knots, dropping like a rock and the ship is shaking violently.

At about half a football field length from touch down I begin a long, very *hairy* flare, pointing the nose to the sky to s*udden stop* the ship. I can see only blue sky through the windshield and have to watch my landing spot out my side and through the Plexiglas chin bubble just in front of my feet.

The ship is light and handling well. And I've already logged more hours in combat than I had driving my '57 Chevy around Southern California before the war. I am very, very good at this. Remember, a little bravado can go a long way in the evil face of danger.

We fall to the ground and slide about a foot, hitting our mark precisely. There are green and white tracers snaking out of the tree line from Chinese and Russian-made automatic weapons ammunition.

Great volumes of American made orange tracers from our infantry, surge back into the trees. The gunships overhead blast rockets and short bursts of minigun rounds into the tree line.

Suddenly, three GI's hop up out of the elephant grass ten feet or so out the right side. They run and stumble toward my aircraft. The two outside grunts have their arms around the middle guy supporting him, carrying him to the ship.

I'm watching temp and pressure gauges on my instrument panel while looking at incoming rounds of fire. And why I ever looked back I'm not sure. It was my first medevac as an Aircraft Commander.

When I turn to look, I'm sickened and horrified to see the young squad leader, Sgt. Sandy Johnson, lying there with both legs gone. A

Viet Cong mine blew one leg off at the knee and the other almost at his hip. Blood is everywhere. The medic is covered with blood and it's being blown all over the inside of the ship. I swear I can taste it.

Sgt. Johnson's hands are clenched into fists, held tight to his sides. I look at the young leader's face. His teeth are clamped so tightly his gums are white.

I'm not sure what registered on my face, but he saw me looking at him. And, for my benefit, he managed a ghastly, horribly distorted grin. I wished he hadn't.

Then, he slowly turned the fist closest to me, and he gave me...a thumbs up sign.

To this day I wished I had never seen it.

Wished I didn't see it again just now.

I nearly lost it. I tried to grin back reassuringly. Then, I turned away, not wanting him to see how I really felt. I'm sick to my stomach and feel weak in his presence. Is this courage or insanity? He had to have had courage to go into combat knowing this could happen. But it will take a different kind of courage now, not knowing what a long life without legs will require of him. And at nineteen or twenty with immediate surgery, he could have a very long life ahead of him.

My crew chief hollers, "Let's go!" and we're off again. I swear I'll get him to the hospital in time if it's the last thing this airplane and I ever do. I push the ship right up to its structural speed limit. Stayed low-level, three or four feet off the deck, all the way so we wouldn't waste time climbing to altitude.

THE HEALING

I wonder if despite his pain, his memories are plaguing him yet. Thanks to morphine, memories in fact could be even more painful to him right now than his wounds. I wonder if all the times he ever used his legs might be coming back to him. The running times. The walking times. The football and baseball times. A park. A girl. A picnic. The beach. All these thoughts must be crowding and hurting him now.

The beach would be especially painful. A football game in the crisp, warm sand, his feet kicking up buckets of sand at a time like small storms as he powers through the line. I wish he would slip into unconsciousness until we get him to the hospital. He doesn't.

He stays awake, grimly gritting his teeth. It takes us just twelve minutes to cover the twenty-four miles to the field hospital pad. I see him wince just a little as they carry him gently into surgery. A very small concession to an enormous, indescribable pain.

We sit on the medevac pad with the huge turbine at idling rpm for longer than we should. My crew and I sit in the relative quiet and stifling heat. We're all waiting for my decision to fly again.

My screams to myself don't violate the silence. At this time in his life, he didn't have that coming! A man this far removed from everything real and meaningful and loved, fighting someone else's god-damned war deserves better than that. His parents shouldn't even have birthed him and raised him for eighteen years just to have him thrown away in this stupid, misguided war.

My first day as an Aircraft Commander and I wanted to go somewhere and throw up. Or cry. Or quit. I want to escape this land of traumatizing days and constant death. But deep down, I know I'll have to keep at it as long as I can. As long as I believe I'm doing this so "freedom might experience a resurrection in this land." Or at least, for as long as I can keep convincing myself that's what we are really doing here.

Besides, I'm convinced all militaries, all governments in all wars count on this…it's personal now… Personal. Never again will war be an abstract. I've been baptized by fire and seen my countrymen murdered with no mercy.

I run the Huey to full power, do a shaky takeoff and climb almost absent-mindedly to optimum altitude. As I approach home base I hear my co-pilot reporting in for me. He shows promise, "Hornet three-three-alpha to base. Medevac mission accomplished. Status-Available. Switching to Cu Chi tower. Out."

Medevac missions in the future would never be the same. We did many. Despite the medevac companies on standby, ready to assist, ready to go in under fire, flying deliberately unarmed helicopters with that big Red Cross as their only shield. We were already there. Already in the shit anyway.

But I never, ever looked in the cargo bay again when picking up our wounded. Never again looked back at what was going on or who we were picking up. Just waited to hear my crew chiefs' "All clear, let's go!" Never looked back there again.

Flying on Pan Am Flight 001 I couldn't wait to get to Lebanon. Now I couldn't wait to leave it. Happy to finally hear the plane was topped off. We could leave troubled Beirut. Felt a sense of relief when we were cleared to the runway. Rumbling our way down the rough taxi-way I couldn't wait to hear us power up and lift off. The sky was freedom. This day it would also be sanctuary.

Often between points on the globe flying was a pleasant quiet time to just think. Nothing outside to see anyway at 30,000 feet. Travel then was a gift, a pleasure, not the drudgery it's become with narrow seats, inconsiderate, self-centered fellow travelers and small, difficult bags of bad peanuts.

All the seats on the early 707 were leather, big and roomy. The food service was on real china with actual silverware. Dining choices were four to five stars. Steaks were freshly cooked made to your order, liquor included. No extra fees or charges for anything. Stewardesses were stunning, friendly, and they pampered you.

Being airborne was in a sense an asylum. It became a time when you could think and perhaps digest, ingest what you might have learned from the people in the last country you visited. A time to put things in perspective. Inhale and embrace whatever new meanings or understandings about the other people on this planet you had just learned. All the while there was that other voyage happening on a level I still had not yet recognized.

Of course, there was no need for airport security or screening then. Wish you all could have been there. The airline staff was warm and welcoming, helpful, knowing the success of their airline depended on it. Still it was more than paycheck. There was pride and professionalism. So staying on the plane wasn't uncomfortable.

A tall, slender, long legged stewardess came by soon after departure from Beirut. She offered me a drink. She was attractive but looked like she could use a drink herself. Ever chivalrous, I offered her one of her own drinks. Maybe I wasn't entirely alone in my worry sitting down there on the tarmac. She said she hated this route. Beirut was always a dreaded stop over and the airline made the entire crew stay on the plane there. We had added some new passengers at the airport. They melted into available seats, stiff, tense and alert. Seemed after a while they relaxed with the relief of successfully leaving that conflicted country.

Pretty sure my sense of fear was exacerbated by my time in combat. But you didn't need that experience to be troubled by heavily armed soldiers in close proximity.

India...

I BELIEVE MUMBAI was mispronounced "Bombay" for well over a hundred years. This because the egocentric English during their expansionism in the mid-1800s simply couldn't pronounce it properly. Of course, they thought that it was the indigenous people who didn't pronounce it properly.

The main boulevard into Mumbai had beggars lined often three and four deep, vying for space, all with their hands out. I had never seen this before anywhere I'd ever been. This heartbreaking visual lasted all the way from the airport to the hotel. At the hotel, the ills and pain of the outside world were barred from entry. The huge two-story hand-carved doors in the lobby kept the outside reality at bay.

An early James Bond movie had convinced me to travel five-star. Custom tan, belt leather luggage, custom made shirts, shoes, cashmere sweaters and four to five-star accommodations. Expensive but the luxury felt pretty damn good.

Amazing to watch the citizens of this city, a mix of Buddhist, Hindu and Muslim going through the marketplaces downtown. All shopping for food, water and life's other very same essentials. Equally essential to each of them. Yet their religions so diverse, a couple belief systems even diametrically opposed. How is it we can shop side-by-side for our daily bread, yet we are unwilling to admit or address our basic commonality?

The human need for religion has spawned so many separate and disparate beliefs. Each to our own embraced belief systems we allow these accepted paradigms to govern our very lives. Our decisions, actions, and non-actions.

Most on this planet have adopted one of the major monotheistic deity systems. I will never. I lost any semblance of belief in the god myth in Vietnam. The old bromide, "There are no atheists in foxholes," sounds good but so wrong. I became an atheist dropping soldiers out of a helicopter onto jungle battlefields.

Atheism isn't the absence of joy or contentment. It's the absence of delusion. Being an atheist, you don't have a book or a group delivering mandates for behavior or eternal consequences for how well you did. It offers cleanly the perspective that we have just this one life and only a limited time to do good things, help others, hopefully spread goodwill and try for a peaceful world. So, we better get about it daily, love our lives and all others, right now.

Likely amazing to any religious still reading but the non-religious can have as much good will toward others and hearts filled with love and compassion for all.

Being human requires high levels of compassion, deep reservoirs of understanding.

As I strolled that market it occurred to me that maybe there's something my journey is showing me. I was staggering through the world alone but buoyed up by the unsolicited welcome warmth of others. The young girl in Thailand would only be the first of many to show me the way back. It hadn't all sunk in yet, hadn't changed me that I could see or feel or even yet know. But I was learning.

Other beings on this planet recognized me as another life form just like themselves. Universally, they would then simply offer hope, succor, warmth and acceptance.

In Vietnam I watched the best and worst of human nature claw its way out of each of us daily. Human nature…not the Devil with scaly skin and a bifurcated tail representing evil: the worst of our nature. And not God, the icon of our good side. No cause and effect by omniscient forces or supernatural beings outside ourselves. Just pure, unadulterated human nature. All from within. Within each of us.

The innate savagery available to the human heart is staggering. The great reservoir of moral justification for inhuman, inhumane acts on one another is impressive and at once deeply, deeply troubling. Mystifying.

Illogical anyway that an omniscient being, "Created us in his own image." A perfectly great fabrication and construct for the archetype model; sheep need a shepherd. Perfectly great fabrication and construct for obeisance to a higher power. But then, paradoxically, it puts us in a world where we each believe our own theology, our concept of God and patronage to same is the right one. And all others wrong.

So let the games and bloodshed begin.

What's really out there? On the other side? Seems a shame to think there's nothing at all, doesn't it. Nothing going on after our death? After we shed these mortal coils? Humans can't accept that. We as a species, as egocentric beings, refuse to accept that this elaborate consciousness we think refined and so valuable just ends.

So, we conjure up the myth of life everlasting, in heaven or hell. And without ever knowing the reality of it, totally on faith, embrace it until we are dead. But before we leave this life and do know what's coming we find ourselves commissioned, exhorted to perpetrate our beliefs on other people, other lands, other faiths and the next generation. We convince one another at churches, synagogues and mosques that this, here and now isn't it. This life is only rewarded later, when we're dead, in a five-star land beyond our ken as mere humans.

But this is it! The great joy day by day, moment by moment, is life. Our lives. To what purpose cries out the ever-stalwart logic? Plato and Socrates believed our reward for a life well-lived was simply a life, well-lived.

The basic belief in an afterlife is an assumption taken on faith. It's based on millennia, eons of myths being retold over campfires even before the first written language. Told over and over by mere mortals like ourselves who haven't yet been to the other side either. There must exist a finer place as our just desserts for the life well lived.

Can't believe that if I don't follow the rules and buy into one of the vended religions I'll end up roasting on the same spit as Hitler, Stalin or Pol Pot. Seems extreme for fudging on an expense report.

And looking around the streets of Mumbai I don't understand why all these people need to even believe in life eternal. And further believe that only *their* chosen path will get anyone to that pleasant, rewarding afterlife. Most believe those choosing other paths are doomed to an afterlife in Hell rather than Heaven. Sad. Shameful.

Australia...

STAYED IN SYDNEY for a while in a great hotel. It was a tall, round, white building in an area known as King's Cross. First morning there in a cafe across the street an attractive waitress poured my coffee and asked me out for dinner and a play...that night! While she filled my coffee cup! Just like that. Forward, aggressive. She was obviously the blatant hussy mom had warned me about. I'd been looking for her ever since. Stayed in that country longer than I planned.

One thing led to another rather quickly. But I was surprised to discover afterwards, lying in bed together, I seemed to take more pleasure from holding her than I ever had before with anyone. Beyond the stirring in the loins something else was stirring. There was another need, another striving making its presence known.

We both knew I wasn't staying in Australia. It was just sex between two healthy humans satiating each other's needs. I don't remember being especially affectionate as a teenager before the war with girls after lovemaking. I certainly wasn't with the prostitutes in the R&R cities the military checked for us. The Army doctors, worried as ever about our health, checked the girls for disease and issued cards. It was purely business with those girls. They were masters of both the act and the business and business was brisk.

Experience with women my first tour was limited to my imagination. Not many women ventured into the combat areas. A high point in the day of a helicopter pilot in our unit was a day off. They came rarely. A day off didn't mean you didn't fly - you just didn't fly combat. It meant a single ship, "Ass and Trash" mission. A euphemism for hauling people and cargo around the firebases. You would take ammo to a firebase or outpost, walking wounded from a medevac hospital to the bigger hospital at the main air base, guys on emergency leave and Donut Dollies.

As a morale builder the amazing Red Cross sent women to provide coffee, donuts and cheer to the troops. The Donut Dollies as they were dubbed also reminded us of what we were fighting for. Or at least why we were fighting to get back to America. They offered memories from home. They wore dresses and their legs were wonderful.

Everyone expects that when you're near a large idling helicopter there will be turbulence generated from the spinning main rotor blade. Not however if the pitch in the main blades are flat. Among all the things passed on from older combat pilots to new pilots was the nuance of putting a little pitch into the main blades if a Donut Dolly was anywhere near your idling aircraft. To watch them try unsuccessfully to hold down their skirts or dress against the turbulence and lift was a joy to see. Sigh.

It was during my second tour well away from the front lines as General Creighton Abrams' pilot I found myself doing the unexpected; telling a woman no. Refusing an offer of a dalliance for sexual pleasure from an attractive woman seemed odd for me, certainly out of character- but I did it twice. Men will tell each other, "Worst I ever had was great." And usually this was true.

Being in Saigon meant being around admin offices and there were many. It takes a huge amount of logistical support to run a war. Met a young woman, a sergeant in the Army who worked in supply. I took her to dinner one night at one of the amazing French restaurants in Saigon. We were both twenty years old, so it didn't take long to get to the discussion of addressing our physical needs. Mine were obvious. Hers were diabolical. She frankly told me she wanted to get pregnant by me. She had two or three more years to serve and wanted out. She felt she had made a mistake by joining and the fastest way a woman could be discharged from service was to become pregnant. Having raised my younger brothers and sister while our single mom worked to support us, I knew I didn't want kids. The young woman had a plan though. She would get pregnant, get thrown out of the Army then have an abortion. I didn't want any part of that. And should she decide to keep the baby I also didn't want a kid growing up not knowing who their father was. So, I said no. The second time I told a woman no was even more complicated.

Officer's Calls are mandatory meetings in the military. Sometimes they are important. Some are just social. It was at one of these functions in Saigon where I met, let's call her Molly. She was a lieutenant and a trauma nurse. She served at the other end of our medevac missions witnessing the most horrible wounds from screaming, crying, often dying soldiers. She was statuesque and very attractive. I didn't notice at first that she never smiled. My mind was focused elsewhere.

After a couple drinks she suggested we go to her place. She had a small apartment in a military housing building. Her room was bland and dull except for the starched and perfectly ironed military fatigue blouse hanging on the wall. The blouse had four black stars on each shoulder and the name Westmoreland over the pocket. I'm sure General Westmoreland hadn't been there and certainly wouldn't leave his shirt behind if he had. Just an attempt at a little humor.

As we had another drink the mood seemed serious almost, business like. She was on a mission. Abruptly she said, "Let's go to bed." With no apparent joy or interest, she took off her clothes, as did I. The next while we were consumed with each other in pure animal lust. Lust and satiating needs is always a good, but something wasn't right, didn't feel right. When our needs were met she simply said, "Thanks. I got what I needed. There's a taxi on the corner will take you back to your accommodations. Don't promise me anything. Don't call. Just leave."

Unable to muster a cogent response I got dressed and left not knowing what else to do or say. I never called her of course and it took me a while to figure out what had happened.

I saw her once more at another Officer's Call. Eye contact with her was suggestive enough that I realized another quickie could happen. I chose rather to walk away signaling a no, not interested. I felt the woman had apparently been drained of all compassion and warmth. No life left in her just getting through the day meeting her body's most basic needs. Not her fault perhaps through her job of sewing up soldiers, amputating their limbs or declaring them dead. She had become cynical about life and perhaps men in general. I, through the same war, had become a different person and still didn't know what I didn't know. But I knew I didn't want to be intimate with this woman again in an empty, soulless tryst. I think even then I was beginning to recognize a need for more. Later, after the war I seemed to need the human touch, even reaching out for it when I could.

I did stay in Australia longer than I planned. Actually, planning hadn't yet occurred to me. I seem to be floating along, carried forward in a powerful current on a stream of living, of life. Meeting people, seeing new countries and experiencing life after war. When troubled again or when curiosity drove me I would go to the airport and get on Pan Am Flight 001 again. Off to another culture but accepted there too and embraced by the warm gift of humanity.

Maybe there wasn't any outward manifestation of the turmoil inside me. Still, I came to believe I had become a monster. Monsters have no feelings, can witness and even create massive pain and death. They can be surrounded by and dwell quite comfortably in carnage. But maybe only I saw the monster, the non-human I had to be to get through war. Outwardly, maybe my visage was still the young man who, as I had been told, had a nice smile.

The curator of the Sydney Zoo then kept albino animals in his front yard across the bay from the Opera House. Pure white kangaroos, wombats, koalas all free to roam the manicured green lawn right down to the waterfront. I'm sure they're gone. Likely politically incorrect now to keep only white animals in his yard.

Aussies are a warm friendly people. It's one of the places on my travels I felt completely at home. I felt I could settle there, be happy and prosper. But at least then you couldn't immigrate to Australia unless they needed your skill or trade. Imagine telling people you can't stay in their country unless you can contribute to their society? What gall? How politically incorrect can one be? Pilots were stacked up like cordwood after the war, so I couldn't get a flying job there, stateside or anywhere else.

Before I went to Vietnam I was just a happy Southern California kid who liked, hamburgers, sandlot football and the beach. The next clear memory I have is that of being shot at while piloting a large, sparsely armed helicopter into a firefight to pick up wounded American soldiers. I was twenty years old.

Some say, parents and teachers mostly, I was having way too much fun in college. The beach and dirt bikes were getting in the way of higher education. So, the grades dropped. I dropped out, and shortly thereafter, I was drafted. Apparently, I forgot to let the Los Angeles draft board know that I had since moved to Hawaii. Surfing, skin-diving and tall young women vacationing from the Midwest every week. Paradise.

Just surfing in Hawaii before the Army

With my lapse in communication with the draft board though, I gained some time.

The Hawaii board had filled its quota for several months ahead, so I had a brief window to try to get into one of the military flight schools. I made it into the Army Warrant Officer Flight School program. Always wanted to be a pilot. The philosopher who said, "Be careful what you wish for," got it right.

It had all happened so fast. Flight school had been a year of intense education, pressure and thrills. Great flight instructors taught me in the forests of Alabama how to knock a specific pine cone out of a tree with the tip of my main rotor blade while hovering a really big helicopter in a really small clearing.

The small Bell trainer I flew in primary flight school."

Off-syllabus lessons in low-level flying at a hundred miles an hour with my skids in the treetops-built confidence. "You can't just pull back on the cyclic stick to climb," the instructor told me. "If you don't add power as well you will drag your tail rotor through the trees." Army flight school prepared me well. Most Fort Rucker flight instructors had only recently returned from a Vietnam tour in combat. They assured me I'd do fine. Learning to fly was incredibly easy and came naturally for me. Becoming an officer was not as easy, not nearly as natural.

During the Army's intense Primary Flight School, I was busted one morning during one of our regular rigid inspections for having a dirty razor. Couldn't have been that dirty as I was barely even shaving. But I was put on restriction and ordered to report to the Company Commander every morning at 5:30 for "razor inspection." Still dark outside, I met with the Commanding Officer in his office. I stood at solemn attention with my razor held at Port Arms. After the third or fourth early morning of failing his inspections I went to the PX and bought a new "hideout" razor.

Next morning, I reported to the CO again. He studies the razor for a long time. I'm scared he'll figure it out–and he does. Finally, he says, "Perfect. Absolutely clean... And, actually... it looks brand new." Now I know the shit is going to hit my personal fan. He looks me right in the eye and says, "Good for you. You're off restriction."

What? Wow. My blank expression drew no explanation. I figured it out later. Beyond learning to fly and becoming an officer he wanted me to learn how to act if I was shot down and became a prisoner of war.

Always fight back. Never quit. Beat the system. Find a way. Always find a way.

Italy...

HAILED A CAB at the airport, which turned out to be a dingy, really seasoned Fiat. Wanted to see a little of Rome of course on the way to the hotel. And we're off. The cabbie speaks English, or really "American" fairly well. There is a difference. Likely helps in his job.

Thought he would be bored having to do this for several tourists a day. Rather he seems to bubble over with enthusiasm pointing out ancient Roman structures. Some even older than his Fiat.

The art, architecture and culture of this old city make it one of the most amazing centers of civilization in the world. I'm a little tired from the flight, ready for my hotel. My driver though, is reveling in his storytelling and I'm caught up in it.

He looks over his shoulder a lot making sure I see what he is pointing at and that I'm understanding his message. As we slice our way around traffic I begin to believe we're going to die in a horrible collision. The thought of getting killed in a Rome traffic circle after leaving helicopter combat in Vietnam seems morbidly ironic. The cabbie is driving with one hand, gesticulating wildly with the other. Seems oblivious to our imminent death.

Don't remember when it was the cabbie turned off his meter. Seem to have a vague recollection but no acknowledgement on his part or mine that my sightseeing tour had now become his mission, not his fare. What is going on here with this gregarious man? This had happened once before in Sydney. I mentioned to the cab driver there taking me to my hotel he had a cool shirt and asked, "Where did you get it?" "Here, I'll show you mate." He turned off his meter, took me to his favorite men's shop and parked the cab. Then he went in with me and helped me pick out a couple of shirts. Getting close to the hotel again he turned his meter back on.

I would always wonder throughout this journey if I was adopted or embraced so easily so often because I traveled alone. Certainly, never appeared at a cafe or restaurant with built in companionship, already encapsulated in a closed bubble of conversation. Realizing how lucky I was to survive war at all, my aura might be changing. I was perhaps glowing with signals that said, "Thanks for letting me visit your country. You can't imagine the one I left. I'm lucky to be here."

But maybe I appeared just lost or needy somehow. Maybe I appeared a human obviously in need of repair. Perhaps everyone but me could see how I had such a tenuous hold on my own being.

This Italian cabbie makes his living from fares, yet here he was taking time out of his day to openly display his pride in his city and country. I remember I used to be proud of my country too. And it came to me just then, I wanted to be proud again.

I wanted that back. That whole feeling of having a home had dissipated. I had become disconnected from my roots, my entire joyous childhood and growing up easy as an American. I'd been up-rooted, set adrift and wasn't sure where I belonged anymore.

Where is home? What had changed? Where did my pride in America get lost?

I wasn't ashamed of how we acted as soldiers in Vietnam. There were certainly atrocities-on both sides. But those rare incidents aside we acted with honor and fought hard. We tried to win gallantly against both a fierce enemy and a myopic Washington D.C.

I never saw or even heard about an act of cowardice on our side. Bravely fought. But something had distanced me from my comfortable assumptions about my life and my country.

England ...

WAITED IN LINE in a drizzly rain at a London theater to see "Midnight Cowboy." Theatrical film promotion wasn't the art and science it is now. All of us, Brits and me alike, thought we were going to watch an American Western.

Went to the Birmingham Small Arms factory outside London to buy a BSA motorcycle. Told the plant manager I wanted to learn about import/export perhaps as a business career. He said, "Well here's your first lesson, mate." He then had an engineer take my brand-new bike back out of its wooden crate, reassemble it, and drove it around their track for six miles. Sold it to me used. Saved me a bundle on export and import taxes.

He didn't have to do that. So why did he? Perhaps he was just connecting with another human being on the planet as best he could. Shared his wisdom with a complete stranger for no reason other than I guess, what, humanity? Didn't cost him anything. Didn't net him anything but my gratitude.

Higher education comes from the weirdest places.

Somewhere around the shored-up Dickens original bookshop a guy walking the opposite direction on the sidewalk on a London street says, "So how are things in the colonies, mate?" Didn't want anything, just a great opening line. An icebreaker. I guess I just looked American. Wasn't sure I wanted to though.

I wanted to blend in with every culture, mix in, disappear...but

**Taken by a street photographer
while walking around London**

couldn't. Apparently, I was a marked man, an obvious American. Couldn't ascertain the good or bad of this. But there was perhaps a currency then in being American. At that time, in spite of Vietnam, we were still respected as a nation around the world.

In my office there is an eight-edition book collection titled, "The History of the Decline and Fall of the Roman Empire" by Edward Gibbon. I wonder if I should read at least the last volume and see how it ends? So many economic, political and foreign policy mistakes along with rampant corruption the last couple of decades we are no longer on a pedestal internationally.

Flight school and officer training took a year. I took a month off afterward in Southern California then went to Vietnam. I still remember standing about halfway back in the plane waiting behind other soldiers to get off the Boeing 707 at the huge air base outside Bien Hoa. War was such an abstract to me. I remember thinking as I walked to the door to get off the plane that it would be pitch black outside. Even though I knew it was mid-day.

Flying in Vietnam was an education. I knew I was learning a lot about everything. Every day it seems I'd learn something new, about me, life, and human nature. Learned things I never thought I'd know. Learned things I didn't want to know. All of us did. We were all so young.

We weren't just learning about life and death and the shearing, sudden, subtle difference between the two. We were young and learning good reasons for living. We thought we had also embraced equally good ones for dying. Like not wanting to return home crippled for life with missing limbs. Or blind. Or with your nuts blown off like that one guy. Way too many of us did go home in pieces.

This, despite our sincere, "Kill me if I'm wounded" pacts we all made then violated with our co-pilots. On any terms it seemed life was worth the pain.

Very early into your tour in Vietnam insidious, caustic doubts seeped into all your psychic wounds like an acid. Something about this war wasn't right. You couldn't prove it of course. Couldn't even really talk about it much. We were deliberately left out of the discussions and media assault by the military. We couldn't figure it out. But we knew.

If the growing pains endured switching from patriot to cynic, childhood to manhood, fearful to fearless and back again weren't enough, there was the daily drug. It was a free drug with freaky, exhilarating highs and dismal, sea bottom lows. Adrenalin. And something else too. Something that worked you every bit as hard yet didn't have a name. It came with the rock and a hard place question: if this war feels so wrong, why do I feel so good? So vital? So important?

With time, looking back I can see through the dichotomy. It's natural enough to be excited about having your own nimble, powerful helicopter when you're only nineteen or twenty. Taking that aircraft into the middle of a firefight to save a soldier's life is an adrenaline explosion, a rewarding and life altering act: for myself and hopefully whomever we picked up out of the fray.

Hearing an emergency radio call for a medevac, knowing you're close enough to answer that call is an incredible rush. You could pass on it. You could even pretend you didn't hear it. You're the Aircraft Commander. The other teenagers on your plane, your co-pilot, crew chief and door gunner can't call you on it. But someone's wounded or otherwise in the real deep shit…and they need you.

The reason they're wounded is because right now they're taking fire. It's likely infantry in a firefight or a downed aircrew with the enemy closing in. Getting them out immediately to medical care means you're going to take fire going in after them. Still, you go. I was important beyond my years. There's a price though.

And, it turns out, a deferred payment plan as well.

With time, some slow healing and distance, I can see I had developed a love-hate relationship with that war. I truly wished I'd never gone. And certainly, I wish I'd never seen some of the things I saw there.

Yet, I wouldn't trade the experience for anything.

When I see a teenager today all buzz haircut, baggy pants halfway down his ass, acne, tattoos and skateboards, I shiver. We couldn't have been thrown into that hellish nightmare when we were really that young could we? Aside from Robert McNamara who at a late date decided to either clear the air or purge his conscience with his book, what were the rest of the politicians, leaders and self-proclaimed statesman thinking? Really, we were still just children.

Scotland…

UNLIKE AMERICA, IF you are by yourself anywhere in Europe at a pub or café you won't get a table to yourself. You might if it's slow. But as meal time approaches, as the crowd increases, if another single comes in, the host or maître de introduces you to someone you've never met. And you share your table with a wonderful stranger, possibly a new friend.

Americans are incredibly territorial. Test it. You step on an elevator in America it's your territory. One other person comes on at another floor and you shuffle and divide the elevator floor space exactly in half. Another comes on and you all move, dividing the elevator floor into thirds. Not an indictment, just an observation.

Other country's people stand closer. Here we would take offense.

Scotland was an entire country of new friends. Felt very much at home there. Could even be home. After all, my Dad was adopted. Who knew his background, his ancestry? That feeling of being at home might have to do with race memory. Recently through Ancestry.com I found my earliest ancestors were originally from the area of Ireland then migrated to Newfoundland. Dad and his brother were orphans left on the porch of an orphanage in Maine. Mom's side was French-Canadian from Newfoundland. I'm told I'm one-eighth Micmac, a Native American tribe in Maine where I was born. Not at all sure what the fraction means.

After getting past the thick, lyrical accents I discovered a slew of new folks trying to understand me and the war. Didn't know it yet but they, trying to understand me, helped me. That wasn't their goal of course. But it came about and developed as they kept asking questions. They kept drilling deeper forcing me to do the same. I was getting closer to the old me. Somewhere inside me still was the kid who didn't think he had an enemy in the world...and didn't until sent to war.

Greece...

SPENT AT LEAST a week there. Okay, much more I think. Wonderfully warm people and culture. Dancing and Ouzo... Their outlook on life glowed like smiles above their heads. Don't these people ever stop dancing and drinking? Even the chubby, swarthy waiter at an outdoor café seemed to lightly dance, float and hum as he went from table to table. Content and happy...I'm envious.

How do I get back there from where I am now?

I knew I wasn't happy anymore. Some things came to me quickly on this journey. A good example was discovering I wasn't happy. Other things took longer to perceive and understand like broken bones needing time to heal. But happiness... reasons to smile or think wonderful thoughts wasn't an effort before. Now it's a laborious, tedious task. The obvious wasn't any longer available to me.

The most natural endearing sights: two people walking on a beach holding hands, children laughing and playing catch, puppies chasing each other...were all blocked. Nothing broke through the boundaries of perception I'd put up. Nothing got in. Nothing could get to me.

I wouldn't allow it. I was protecting myself from a disorder; war. A war that no longer existed for me. But there was a void, a vacuum, an empty space where happiness and contentment used to live. Could be its chewed up or crushed forever. Or maybe just lurking around a hidden revelation or epiphany, playing hide and seek with me. I wonder if I can find them again. They were deeply embedded in me before. Taken for granted from childhood in America, I grew up with them.

THE HEALING

In Greece I stayed in a pure white village overlooking an azure sea. I can't remember the name, but the old village was built like swallows build nests in caves and under bridges. Little homes had common walls, almost communal. The boutique hotel I stayed in was built the same, separated only by a cobblestone walkway and dirt path, from buildings on either side.

I'll never know what the villagers saw in my eyes. Could they see I needed healing? Did they know I needed to be embraced as a human and welcomed back into the fold? Was it obvious I needed to be told, "All is well. Everything is going to be okay again someday. You're going to be okay."

And if my need was so obvious, so visible, why did they feel they should help? Why bother? Do not know why for sure. Suspect they just reached out to a stray needing some attention. Whatever the reason, they did reach for me.

Not sure what frightening visage they saw in me. But what I saw in their eyes was acceptance and welcome. I had changed so much I felt the monster. Unlikely, unseemly things had been growing inside me and festering for over a year. Belief and value systems had become corrupt with the bankruptcy of human kindness that is war. I didn't know how or even that I needed to reach out for help. I was bereft of feelings. Overdrawn on trust and understanding as currency. But strangers kept making donations and deposits into my account.

The innate kindness in people everywhere shone like beacons.

If I were a ship at sea on a stormy night I'd see lighthouses.

They were everywhere.

Total strangers asked, "How are you?" Then waited patiently for my answer.

I was beginning to slowly understand. Something was happening on a level I wasn't totally privy to yet. But I began to recognize the fact that I had stopped feeling anything. Anything at all. I was numb.

It was likely a subconscious choice for my survival. Don't remember exploring it, debating with myself, "Should I or shouldn't I go comatose for the rest of this war?

Becoming numb had likely saved my sanity while at war. I don't see how anyone can witness carnage on any scale and not shut down some of their perceptive sensors. It would be a data overload of dangerous proportions. First few days watching other aircrews get shot down or young soldiers get killed you were horrified. But you couldn't stay in that altered state. Dangerous to linger there. You had to get past that so you could survive and operate successfully in that environment. We had a job to do.

Don't remember when I stopped being horrified at the carnage around me.

But pretty sure I stopped feeling anything at all that same day. Stop feeling. And go to a dark place in your heart for the rest of your tour just to get through it.

But everywhere I went on this globe after the war total strangers tried to make me understand I couldn't stay there. Shouldn't. I didn't need to be numb anymore. As a matter of fact, staying numb would deny me the full privileges and benefits of being human. This was true everywhere I traveled.

Not far from my hotel I could see into the courtyard of a small tidy home. For the time I was there a ritual formed. I anticipated it, waited and watched for it like a predator, a raptor on high from my hotel balcony. Dinnertime, late evening, the day cooling, a family of five would sit at the table in their courtyard to eat, Mom, Dad and three children just eating together.

Too far to hear and lip-reading was out so I imagined, "What did you learn in school today?" "How did work go today dear?" "How did tryouts go today for soccer?" Family questions. Caring questions. Home questions.

France…

FELT TOLERATED IN Paris–not welcome really. The French allowed me to eat in their restaurants and bistros, drink their fine wines, allowed me to enjoy their landmarks and scenery. But I was ignored. Not forcibly or verbally ostracized, just ignored. Sooner I left their country the better was the only thing I imagined we would all agree on.

On the flight out of Paris I met an Army Special Forces Sergeant. He was going home after his second tour in Vietnam. When I got on the plane despite the full-dress uniform with four rows of battle ribbons on his chest it seemed no one else saw him. Or maybe didn't want to see him. Didn't want to engage in a conversation. Could be, like a lot of folks then, they might not want to hear what he had to say. People kept moving past him without looking at the empty seat next to him. So, I sat there.

He had been wounded at the Battle of Kham Duc. That fight was the most ferocious and intense combat the Vietnam War ever saw. It was also one of America's worst losses. Several thousand North Vietnamese soldiers overran a small American Special Forces outpost. With close quarter fighting and hand to hand combat 259 American and South Vietnamese soldiers were killed, hundreds more wounded. 31 American soldiers were deemed Missing in Action in only the first 24 hours. Eight aircraft were shot down trying to help the guys on the ground. All in just forty-eight hours.

The wounds he had from Kham Duc were serious enough he needed nearly a year to recover. Probably could have been medically discharged but insisted on staying in. Then he insisted on another tour.

Wanted to go back and fight. That's Special Forces for you. He was quiet at first in his own world, his own pain. Respectful when we introduced ourselves then quiet again. By the time Pan Am Flight One was on its leg out of Paris he had been in eleven countries. I asked him when he left Saigon?

His cryptic response was, "Couple days ago."

Then I was quiet. I had been stopping often, learning, discovering along the way. And the hard, dark shadows at the edge of my being were gently being chipped away by complete strangers I met everywhere. I hadn't asked them to. Inherently, no matter the color of their skin the human race just needs and wants the same things; acceptance. Understanding. Love. And the natural instinct is to show and offer those traits before receiving them. He wasn't going to let anyone show him anything until he had dragged all his baggage and horror back home. He would deal with it there when he finally figured it out.

Had to say something so I said, "You gotta get off the plane."

The statement startled him, brought him back to the present with me. He said," What?"

I said, "You gotta get off this plane. Next stop. Promise me okay?"

"For what? I just want to get home."

"I know. So do I. But you can't just jump out of Hell, leave that environment abruptly and carry all the pain home with you. We've been in a place no one should ever have to go. It's an enormous chasm away from where we should be now."

"Not sure what you mean?" he said.

"Not sure myself yet," I responded slowly. "But I'm starting to understand some things. Look, there's a bunch of people, all strangers in fact, out there in nearly every country we land in that would like to show you and me the way back. I didn't get it at first. But these strangers reach out to pull me back from the edge almost everywhere I stop." Funny but until I voiced this to him I hadn't seen my own journey with such clarity. We have bridges to build and cross throughout life. Coming back from a war to life as we envisioned it wouldn't be easy without help.

"Way back to what?" he wanted to know.

"Normalcy? Real life I think. Life in America? Home? Not sure but no one should have to go where we were, where we've been. Now we have to go back to life without killing and the danger of dying if you don't kill. No one wins a war, everyone loses. But if you've been in a war you lose more than the rest. You and I aren't who we think we are anymore. Not who we were. And we got a long way to go. I only just learned that from others on this planet."

The stewardess stopped at our aisle first and said to him, "What do you need soldier, I'm buying." It brought a tiny smile to his face since he knew the drinks were free. We both recognized that she had passed everyone else to serve him first. Maybe to honor his service sprawled like a colorful garden of battle ribbons and medals across his chest. Maybe he wasn't as far gone as I was. Maybe he was tougher than me. Still, talking to him was helping me in a weird way.

"And listen, when you get home and things aren't what they seem, don't quit on us, the rest of us. Don't give up. If you start to wonder where humanity is buy as many Billie Holiday records as you can find and listen to her. Then reach out to the rest of us. We're there for you. ...But, you gotta get off the plane, man."

Ireland…

WHY IS IT every culture figures out a local vegetable or plant to distill and ferment to create booze? Who thought of it first? Had to be an accident the first time. Something mistakenly gets left out and turns. Some caveman smells it, thinks it smells good and dares Neanderthal Ned to try drinking it.

Ned then gets shitfaced but happy and funny, finally showing some personality. And the word spreads. Potatoes become vodka in Russia. Cactus is Mexico's solution to sobriety. Somewhere in history as humans spread throughout the world this phenomenon caught on.

I remember one morning leaving a pub in Belfast. It was raining, and I wasn't prepared. Should have been. Knew it was looking like rain when I left the hotel. Come to think of it, it looked like rain the entire time I was there. But, no umbrella or other rain gear, nothing.

Another stranger walking by saw my dilemma. So, on a whim, from some well of kindness or simple humanity inside him, he offered to share his umbrella to his next stop. As luck would have it, another local pub. We walked together nearly arm in arm sharing his tiny shelter from the rain.

Arriving at another warm, inviting tavern up the street I was introduced to the gathering there. For the next while in that wonderful happy building, I couldn't buy my own drinks. I learned two important things there that night.

First, the intricacies of mixing real Irish Coffee. Properly done more complicated than you might imagine. Spoon held just under the surface of the coffee pouring rich, real cream into the spoon just as it breaks the surface, so it spreads beautifully into a thick layer over strong coffee and excellent Irish whiskey at the bottom.

After one of those artful creations though, I switched drinks. Went back to the aged, single malt Scotch I had discovered in Scotland.

More importantly, I also embraced the fact that humans everywhere feared and at once cherished all the same things. Doesn't matter if you live in a penthouse overlooking the Thames or a grass hut barely clearing the mangroves over a swamp in Sumatra.

I was to be reacquainted with this very basic concept of being a human all over the world. Kept relearning it anew every stop around the planet. I was being reintroduced to humanity from the ash covered, inhuman landscape of war by my fellow humans. I was handheld, comforted and counseled by total strangers everywhere I went. Most didn't know perhaps they were helping me at all. But their innate kindness, their welcoming me to their country and often their homes and families was cathartic. They couldn't know the reparations they were enabling in me. But I was starting to feel things again...strange that I had forgotten or disabled lifelong certitudes to get through the chaos.

No one hated me, and I hated no one. I had friends everywhere I went. And only had enemies in one small beautiful country in Southeast Asia by political mandate.

Spain...

THERE ARE NO real language barriers. People can communicate if they wish: sign language, pointing at objects, yelling. Though, repeating yourself louder and louder doesn't really help.

Met a family on a Spanish beach who just swept me up into their life for a couple days. They were from Portugal over on holiday. The little tribe's mother was the real outgoing one. She epitomized the title, "Matriarch."

Everyone deferred to her will or instructions, including me. She would order food at restaurants for her husband and two kids. With a look at me she would also order for me, which was helpful, delightful actually. Not even uncomfortable since I couldn't read the menu at the non-tourist cafes we frequented anyway. Then she would decide for everyone it was time to take a walk on the beach but too early to go in the water. She was heavyset. No, wait. She was fat.

And given so easily to that magical human gift of touching and smiling and hugging and laughing. What a life force filled with passion and kindness. What a tremendous gift this woman was to everyone on our entire planet. And especially just then, to me.

I relished the touch and warmth of others. I think my handshake greetings with others were longer than they needed to be. Even being jostled in a crowd made me smile. I'm sure this woman's life was filled with responses in kind everywhere she went from everyone she ever met in her life. Hope so.

THE HEALING

Don't remember her name. Will never forget her touch.

She taught me how to hug, really. It isn't a grip on your shoulders or patting your back. The word describing a hug best is *engulfing*. Arms overlapping in back, heads bowed, side-by-side, ear-to-ear, touching one another. Can't get closer to another fully dressed. The proper hug isn't over until that person knows they are safe or loved or cherished or have been truly missed.

She basically adopted me, treating me as a child of hers for the time we spent together. Of all the things I was beginning to miss about America, family was topping the list. I knew they would accept me, as is, no matter what. No matter what I'd become.

They had to, right? That's what family is for, what it's about. I had traveled so far away from who I was, who they thought I was, they might not know me anymore. Still I felt the need to decompress. More time, meet more people, see new countries. Or maybe just resolve some things before I saw family again.

Or maybe get closer to me again before I foisted myself on my family.

I was alienated from me, from who I thought I was or should be. It was an uncomfortable realization.

Africa...

GOT INTO A pickup football game on the beach somewhere on the African coast. Watched for a while on what were the apparent sidelines. Teams became uneven and one of the players simply waved me over. We drew plays in the sand with our fingers. Pointing at me meant I was to run this line in the sand. Just like home, America, full speed, full-tackle, no pads or equipment. "Shirts versus skins" to designate teams.

Began to feel homesick for a younger time and a better place. But I'm sure they were both gone. Can't ever go there again. And I'm not really ready to go back home yet either.

I had played well enough in college to get asked to try out for the Coca Cola semi-pro football team. The offer wasn't based on scholastic play but rather our amazing and highly organized sandlot games played at city parks all around Pasadena. Between dirt bikes in the California desert, football and helicopters it's amazing I survived my own youth.

I could see a vague similarity between football and war. Both release and rely on primitive caveman instincts. Both rely on strategies and tactics. One is often instantly gratifying like when you knock a defensive back on his butt and blow past him for a touchdown. The other is not rewarding on any level except if you live through another day of combat.

I weighed the football offer against a friend who had an apartment in Hawaii with an extra room. Stay in LA and get the crap kicked out of me as the quickest but smallest guy to ever play semi-pro football... or go to Hawaii and surf...hmmm?

I believe it was that first five-hour flight across the Pacific realizing how far I had to travel to get to Hawaii where I was first bit by the travel bug. What a planet.

Pakistan...

EVERYONE IN KARACHI seems angry. Or is it me? Maybe this reflects my own anger. Anger was the common emotion in combat. Fear went away soon after flying into combat. Replaced by a calm acceptance of your likely death approaching a landing zone to pick up infantry. Replaced as well by adrenalin.

No. It's not me. Karachi is crowded, hot, unattractive, with limited choices for food or drink. There is an acknowledgment, a begrudging acceptance apparently that this is life as good as it gets with few ways to improve it. There's nothing really but desert outside the city limits where all the little streets defer to one road.

I'm uncomfortable here. These people are uncomfortable with me judging by the unguarded looks of disdain I see and feel.

I grew and learned on my travels becoming closer to me and perhaps purging some demons. I've learned in the years since that my journey was only to begin a lifelong quest of finding myself. Just like everyone does. Bit of a side trip not everyone takes with the war and a slow trip around the world perhaps.

But all of us search, learn and grow.

Today, the excitement and most of the pain is gone. There are memories to deal with though. Still and for always, I guess. Assigned to the 116th Assault Helicopter Company at Cu Chi after flight school my pilot education began all over again as a newbie. We were called Peter-Pilots, a pejorative term for a lowly co-pilot.

In that unit you had to have around 300 hours in combat and the unanimous positive vote of all the Aircraft Commanders in your platoon to make AC yourself. I switched to the left seat as AC with 270 hours. My first co-pilot ever was Charlie Danielson. He was next in line to make AC, the most senior co-pilot. He and I had arrived at Cu Chi the same day and became friends. My first mission was a nine-ship combat insertion.

As a new AC you flew the last ship in the flight of nine or, what we called Eagle Flights, of less than nine aircraft. This Tail End assignment was in case your formation flying wasn't fully developed or fully trusted yet. Tail End was also the designated medevac ship for the obvious ability to break out of formation easily without interrupting the flight.

Returning alone to a hot landing zone as a new AC for those first medevacs are seared into my consciousness. Moment by moment I still fly those early missions almost daily. Some grunts are dragging most of what was an American soldier, a kid my age, on board my aircraft. And there's so much blood. It's everywhere. Picked up by rotor turbulence and flung diluted all over the aircraft–it turns pink. It's on windshields and gauges, flight suits, hands and memories.

It's so ugly, real and scary that the boy who loved burgers and beaches hides under the covers in the back of his mind. Flying in combat, I learned to drink just so I could sleep. Subconsciously, I soon learned to cauterize my emotional system to avoid being wounded, healed and wounded again.

The carnage and trauma hit you so fast and so hard there was no time for scabs to form anyway. I was flying right out of my childhood at 110 knots, four feet over the rice paddies of a country I didn't know in a war I didn't understand.

Nothing I had ever done, learned, read, watched, or believed prepared me for the days ahead or the years to follow. And absolutely nothing prepared me for the lingering daily, crystal clear memories that are still not getting fuzzy around the edges. That year and a half changed me forever.

In some ways I believe I'm better for it. What I learned about myself, human nature, and value of life has shaped many decisions and attitudes since. Treat every day since the age of nineteen as a gift and it will impact your life. There's a price to be paid for that education, however. I'm still paying tuition.

At times awakening too early or too fast, caught mid-dream for a second or two, I lie in bed grappling with a dream-like reality. "Where am I?" It takes a second or so to separate myself and my immediate surroundings from the warm womb of sleep. In these first few vulnerable seconds I'm always in limbo. Coming from that moment of sleep into reality in Vietnam always resulted in a door slam flash of panic, "What will happen today? What will I do…or see?"

Panic would then ebb. Logic would take charge and my day would begin. A mix of logic, instinct, excellent training and fear pervaded my every action in combat. There is not a more dependable coalition of processes to assure survival. When all are fine-tuned, working in concert, your odds for survival as a pilot in combat are vastly improved.

There are times these powers or senses and a fine aircraft are all that stand between living and dying. The people at the Lycoming Engine and Bell Helicopter companies should be publicly lauded. They built a flying tank. It was amazing how many bullet holes and damage the Huey would take before it gave up on its crew.

The helicopter combat assaults we did back then were developed specifically for the war in Southeast Asia. Now a proven concept, it's adapted and evolved to fit nearly any war. Simple concept really, soldiers are airlifted instantly by helicopter to any spot on the map. Mobility, speed, and flexibility are the obvious strategic advantages. The complexities of an assault can be broken down into simple steps.

An Assault Helicopter Company would put up as many as nine fly-able troop-carrying helicopters. These are the "slicks," so called be-cause as troop carriers they had little armament, just a couple M-60 machine guns hanging off the side. Two to three heavily armed gun ships would usually go up with us every day. A Light Team was two gunships, a Heavy Team, three.

These gunships were the same Bell-made Hueys as the "slicks." The difference is they are heavily armed with miniguns, rockets, grenade launching cannons and a crew of four spring-loaded to the pissed off position. Their job was simple. Every day go up and kill something. Every day they flew they were hell bent on death and destruction.

The slicks are sent to pick up all or part of an infantry company. If we're hauling American troops this averages out to be about six men, or one squad per ship. While the slicks are loading the troops in a cold pick-up zone, heavy artillery is sometimes "prepping" the land-ing zone with a heavy barrage. This, particularly if it is a "hot LZ," meaning enemy occupied. This prepping is a softening up process used much the same way one might tenderize a steak with repeated blows from a hammer.

On especially tough landing zones this tenderizing is accomplished by bombs dropped from B-52's flying at 30,000 feet or more. You can't see the planes. But on long final to an LZ you can vividly see the bomb concussions splitting the air.

The instant the prepping ceases the gunships move in to suppress any residual resistance. The slicks with their troops are fast-approaching the landing zone. For their purposes the gun ship teams are designed very well. They are morbidly intriguing to watch. A crack gun team will work together like two rows of teeth. The upper and lower rows combine to grab and hold–chewing, gnawing, tearing and applying constant pressure in the right places to keep their prey from escap-ing as they work one high, one or two low, covering each other and blasting hell out of the LZ.

Lots of excitement for a bunch of teenagers who should all be back in America doing teenage things like racing cars and stealing girlfriends from each other. And growing up slowly.

Here's a mission in a capsule. You have four American teenagers per Huey as flight crew. There are about six more American kids as infantry in the cargo bay waiting to step out and mix it up with the bad guys. We're doing 120 miles an hour coming down from fifteen hundred feet in a very tight formation often with our main blades only feet apart. Our only outbound firepower is M-60 machine guns spraying 7.62 caliber rounds out each side of the helicopters.

Two to three Huey gunships are escorting us in. They have rockets, missiles, mortar cannons, miniguns and a crew chief and door-gunner with M-60s. If you take your eyes away from your touchdown point you can see the brown uniforms and pith helmets of North Vietnamese Army regulars running through the jungle toward our touch down point. The noise of machine gunfire and the smell of cordite are unbelievable.

What always amazed me too was how much machine gun fire from both sides never hit anything at all.

Green and white tracers inbound…Russian and Chinese ammunition. American machine gun tracers are orange. On short final behind the gunships a single Huey comes in alone. It's designed to lay down a smoke screen for the landing area commencing a low and slow flight around the perimeter of the LZ.

"Smokey" is equipped with a ring of nozzles that shoots JP-4, a kerosene-like fuel, into the large, hot turbine exhaust. Under these circumstances the fuel doesn't explode. It just burns, becoming a steady, thick cloud of white-grey smoke. The smoke mission was a favorite of mine. Didn't want to fly guns but didn't really like flying in formation either. My family sees this last as a metaphor for my life.

How we flew the "Smokey" mission covering an inbound flight of 116th slicks.

The Smokey mission is a hazardous one. Along with the standard crew chief and door gunner, a roving gunner is used to cover the hot side of the aircraft, the side most likely to take enemy gunfire. Smokey would fly in between the landing flight and whatever tree line seemed to have the most hostile fire. The smoke would obscure the flight on short final making them harder to see, hit and shoot down.

All these separate aircraft and their functions are directed by the "Command and Control" helicopter circling at 2,000 feet above the fracas.

So much for the ghoulish but effective machinations of helicopter warfare. It doesn't speak of the people who lubricate this machine, often with their lives. It does not tell of the human aspect, of emotions. It doesn't speak at all about the intense trauma and extraordinary demand on human capabilities. It says nothing of fear, courage, camaraderie, love, hate, confusion, and frustration, all inextricably knotted together, then stretched taut in a teenaged boy fighting a futile war he believes in less and less every day of his tour.

It says nothing of the faceless names that ordered the battles fought.

Or the nameless faces who fight them.

The term "combat assault" means many things to me. Even now, years later, it means a young pilot I knew who, trapped in his downed aircraft, went insane watching his crew being deviously and horribly tortured by Viet Cong.

It means times of my own intense fear going in under fire to pick up our wounded.

It means at least one of my flight school classmates dying a classic hero's death.

I believe Shakespeare said, later paraphrased by Hemingway, most recently paraphrased by me, "A coward dies a thousand deaths, a hero dies but once." Pete was shot down and had successfully pulled his co-pilot out of their downed and burning aircraft. He then deliberately went back for his crew. He knew the danger. He knew the ship would blow up. Had to.

A downed Huey blows up three times. First the fuel explodes, yellow flames, black smoke. Then the magnesium parts of the transmission explode in a separate white- hot blast. Then, seconds later, all the ammunition explodes or "cooks-off." Every pilot knows this three-step progression which invariably follows when a Huey gets shot down and begins to burn. And Pete's ship was already burning. His co-pilot told me later Pete just looked at the burning wreck, shook his head, said, "Shit!" And ran back into the inferno to get his men. And died with them.

Combat assault to this day means times of my own dread and fear flying over reported radar-guided .50 caliber positions. Whether the reports of that incredible weapon were accurate or not there had been no other route available due to deteriorating weather conditions. I'll never forget the time, still a co-pilot flying "Smokey" that our crew chief was killed, and the door gunner wounded, all within sixty incredible seconds.

It means flying a Huey at 110 miles an hour 2 to 4 feet off the ground, pulling slightly up and flipping it sideways, 90 degrees to the earth, to get through a narrow tree line. This maneuver minimizes your "exposure time," that is, time available as a target to hostile fire. This exposure time did increase if you slowed to gain altitude. But flying sideways for even a few seconds with the rotor blades just clearing the ground was bravado. Folly.

An aspect of military flying is constant training. Helicopters are complex aircraft, so we were always training on emergency procedures. These included: fire on board, hydraulics out, tail rotor failure. And engine-out auto-rotations at altitude, high-speed at low level and hovering. My log showed 200 autorotations to the ground before even leaving flight school.

There was a myriad of things that could go wrong with a Huey but seldom did.

One part of combat flying was breaking in new co-pilots. Co-pilots fresh out of Army flight school serve an apprenticeship. In the 116th we changed co-pilots every day. This dynamic was instituted so they could learn from the hopefully vast reservoir of knowledge, nuance and instinct for survival you as an AC had accumulated. In this unit when you were up for Aircraft Commander candidacy all ACs in your platoon had to vote your approval. We had to absolutely trust each other flying tight formations under fire.

One dissenting vote from any Aircraft Commander killed your chances to become an AC. Some pilots with less than a unanimous vote had to go to another platoon in the company. Some left the 116th altogether.

One day I'm flight lead of a two-ship sortie landing at a fire support base to pick up infantry. There were two pads, side by side, so we would land together. After picking up six American troops for an extended stay in the boonies we would take off single ship, one at a time then form up in the air.

These troops had a lot of gear, rations and ammunition. Even saw one with his puppy. Twice I had picked the bird up, cleared the concertina wire at the edge of the compound turned left over a small river into the wind and nursed the heavy bird into gaining altitude.

Third time coming in to pick up troops I gave the controls to my new copilot, "You have the aircraft." He brings us in fine, empty. The troops get on board; he lifts off, clears the perimeter wire and shocked me by immediately turning right, downwind, right over the river. As a heavy aircraft this is a catastrophic mistake.

All airplanes need to take off into the wind; it adds lift to rotors or wings. Downwind deprives needed lift. I quickly grabbed the controls and per military protocol said, "I've got it." But, he froze on the controls. The next thing I hear on the radio is the second helicopter yelling my call sign, "Three Three, your skids are in the water!"

I nurse the heavy helicopter downwind and upstream for quite a while, trading airspeed for altitude. I was also always fighting with my co-pilot for control yelling at him to take his hands off the controls. I remember vividly the troops sitting in the cargo bay with their feet, their combat boots hanging out the cargo bay just clearing the water. With all their gear if we had crashed into the river they would drown. Stupid way to die in combat.

Finally, we're at 1,500 feet and relatively safe. My co-pilot finally lets go and says something inane like, "Well, we did it." Not much given to profanity I remember lacing into him with language worthy of, maybe even envied by stevedores worldwide. I ended by saying he would never fly with me again. And, if I could manage it, he'd never fly again in this unit or even this war.

Shutting down that night my crew chief told me he had his 45. Caliber automatic pointed at the back of the lieutenant's head. All I had to do was say the word. He knew how much trouble we were in and was willing to kill to save us. Surprised he didn't.

Months later I was now stationed in Saigon flying the Four Star General, Abrams. A beat up, dirty, shot up, bullet holes patched, 116th Hornet ship flew into the pattern at Saigon's heliport, designated Hotel-3. Either the tower or another crew member would always let me know about a Hornet bird in the pattern. Usually it meant the 116th crew had come to tell me one more of my friends had bought it. The Hornet bird had a different mission this time. That lieutenant was up for his vote. I won't divulge his name, but hopefully he never went into aviation as a career. Even though I wasn't officially an AC in that unit anymore they wanted me to vote because of that one mission I flew with him.

Without my crew I flew General Abrams' shiny new helicopter alone up to Cu Chi that night. Good to see everybody of course but the trip wasn't necessary. Wasn't necessary as well over half the other pilots voted against him. He left the unit.

There was also one of the single-ship I flew, resupplying troops out in the jungle after dark. I wish I could truly describe night flying in Vietnam. It's still the only pure black I've ever seen.

Night was unaltered by any man-made light. In clear weather the horizon started where the stars stopped. Now take man's normal fear of the dark, add childlike imaginings of predators and hideous monsters living in the dark, awaiting prey. Then add one very young pilot trying hard for an elusive navigational fix and you have the ingredients that giant fears are made from.

The predators and monsters are real down there, down below in the dark.

If your engine quits, they will own you forever.

Tuning in various radios searching for a fix that night I turned in the Armed Forces Network playing The Doors' *Light My Fire*. The needle pointed to the station giving me direction. I was found again. The hair on the back of my neck stood straight up when I heard that song. It was music from home – California, late sixties. Years later, starting instantly with the one beat, snare drum introduction, the first few bars of the song still gives me chills. Still.

Persia…

I KNOW. BUT the many people I've met from Iran since, always say Persia when asked where they are from. Stopped briefly in Tehran. One of the few places where I didn't feel entirely welcome or at home. Set out to explore anyway.

Cabbie took me down a few winding, tree-lined streets until we hit a roadblock. Not military, just a party that had spilled into the streets. Thought at first it was a masquerade ball. The beautiful traditional costumes indicated to my cabbie we had bumped into a wedding party.

If this was only one wedding it must be for a king and queen. Maybe he was wrong. It looked more like a coronation or some other affair of state. All these people couldn't possibly be related to the bride or groom.

The now suburb of Tehran, really only a neighborhood within the growing urban sprawl, had once been a separate village. It had lost its name but hadn't lost its identity.

Likely there were people old enough to remember the village as it was. Likely the elders never left home when Tehran showed up at their door and engulfed them. In several countries I visited it was not uncommon to find people who had grown up, married, lived and would die within a few blocks of where they were born.

The entire neighborhood for blocks around was celebrating this pairing of families. Such rich pageantry and ceremony for a joining. The bride and groom seemed to glow. The adulation of the crowd was feeding on it. If happiness is an energy this crowd was going nuclear.

Children not yet old enough to even understand marriage were caught up in the celebration and ceremony. Infectious. The happiness of their moms and dads and the whole crowd made them smile and laugh. All hoped for this union to be blessed, filled with contentment and safety for the bride and groom for the rest of their lives. Found myself consciously wishing the same for them. They didn't even know who I was sitting there in the back of a cab watching. But I wanted the best for them.

I hadn't ignored people's messages to me around the world. Never turned away from a handshake or failed to return a smile. But those reactions came easily and at first were only automatic, robotic. There was no real, internal reaction from me. Eventually though, at some point humanity wore me down to a fresh start.

People began to restore my faith in us. They kept trying to welcome me back through so many countries. I began to embrace again being human. With this wedding party spilling over into a dusty street I think I was starting to reach out or perhaps reach back to other humans.

When you have a cold or the flu it's difficult to say when you start to get better. You might be in agonizing discomfort for a few days. But the exact moment you start to heal and feel better is lost, hard to identify. Not sure this wedding was my turn around at all. Just remember feeling something again, for someone else.

It's Easter Sunday, 1969. And it's unlike any I have known before. As I remember Easter Sunday at home, it is an occasion of beauty and serenity, flowers and new clothes, happiness and religious rededication. Easter church services are full of meaning and ceremony. Sure, the choirs of Easter are a little larger than normal. And so are the congregations. But everyone is welcome on this day, more meaningful to Christians than Christmas.

In Vietnam, However, there is no time for services. There is only the mission. But Easter's mission is different.

The mission is to airlift a Vietnamese Infantry Company into a multitude of landing zones patch-worked across Central Vietnam. It is a frustrating and exhausting job as the Vietnamese commanders usually direct us to the wrong landing zones. This lack of planning and organization quite often puts us into "hot" zones that have not been prepped by artillery! Or anything else. After one particularly uncomfortable exercise in this "Vietnamization" of the war, we put the troops out into a "cold" sector and are released until further notice. Our gunships stay behind to protect the infantry troops.

The nine empty slicks head for a village complex known as the Sugarmill.

We had been to the Sugarmill many times before. It's a small, quiet village built around a now defunct mill, surrounded by flat plains and streams. The mill itself is built on the river side of the village, as is the only road to the area. The road, where it is straight, serves as our standby airstrip when working the area.

We land in trail formation, settling to the ground about twenty feet apart. We let the big turbines idle and cool for exactly two minutes, and then shut down. Eight of the other ships follow flight lead at precise two-minute intervals. As Tail End Charlie again, mine is last.

This cooling and shutting down process has the curious effect of going from total noise of engines and rotor blades, to total silence by precise degrees. Usually this transition from combat chaos to comforting quiet is so awesome; there is no talking by the aircrew for a minute or so afterward. It is during this respectful silence that I hear children converging on the ships.

I look up and discover what seems to be hundreds of children milling around the helicopters. There are more kids here than I have ever seen in one place in Vietnam. It's ironic that I should meet so many here on Easter when every other time we'd been to the Sugarmill I don't remember seeing even one.

They were a boisterous but pleasant bunch. They had lean yet soft faces of light brown skin, big dark eyes and blue-black hair speckled with brown dirt and black mud. Perhaps they didn't realize it was Easter. There wasn't a frilly bonnet, pinstripe suit or patent leather shoe among them. Instead, their frail limbs were scantily covered with torn and dirty shorts and now and then ragged shirts as well. Up close, they smell faintly of dried fish and cooked rice. They are pitiful. And lovable.

They are begging for "C-rations" from the weaker-willed men in the company by saying, "Chop, chop G.I.?" And pointing to our emergency supplies strapped under the troop seats. Being an easy mark for this form of extortion, my crew and I give what the ship can spare and enjoy it.

Eventually the sharing turns into a game. The crew thinks it great sport to throw the canned rations across the large mud puddle on one side of the road. Then watch the kids charge through it, racing for the food. There is always something held back for the few who fail the course and tumble laughing, into the warm, shallow puddle.

I sit and think of what is happening at home. Across the dateline

Easter Day has not yet arrived. Everyone will be anticipating the coming day's events.

American children will be anxiously awaiting baskets and egg hunts.

Their parents are perhaps praying for Sunday services while taking a few last stitches on a new little dress. Or sweeping the patio in preparation for company. The roast might already be simmering in the oven.

Young girls will be dying to see their girlfriend's new clothes.

Their boyfriends thinking along the same lines.

Here at the Sugarmill there is a rare, cool breeze blowing. And it's quiet for a change. The land is very green and lush from the heavy rains. There are hundreds of birds in the air, a rarity in this war-torn country. Or maybe I just hadn't noticed them before.

The children are cavorting all over the ships. But this was a welcome, pleasant sound compared to the usual one of guns, artillery and aircraft. At this moment Vietnam is a beautifully serene pastoral. And totally incongruent with the tortured land I had come to know.

Suddenly the peace and beauty are gone – shattered irreparably by a scratchy, distraught masculine voice blasting out of the radio with our call sign: "Hornets! Crank Em up"

In one minute all the children scatter. All the ships are running. In less than two we are flying. The noise is back. The little knot of dread and fear festers once again in my stomach. Those few minutes in what must have been a make-believe land are gone.

THE HEALING

"Lead, this is 'tail-end'. We're up and away!"

"Roger Three-Three," Lead replies with my call sign.

It seems as if I grew up here. As if I have been in this scarred helicopter flying combat missions all my adult life. There's some irony there in that I had been only a teenager when I had arrived. And I felt I'd seen and done enough already to justify being retired or dead.

I notice for the millionth time the bullet hole patches in my windshield. I wonder why they don't give purple hearts to aircraft? I wonder if with all the mangled people will they ever run out of purple? I wonder who picked purple in the first place, and if they had ever been wounded? I'm tired. Tired from tension and fear. And very, very tired of tension and fear.

Camaraderie plays a big part in combat flying. Charlie Danielson and I arrived at Cu Chi, III corps, South Vietnam, on the same day. We shared living quarters, our "hootch" and a makeshift sandbag bunker. We became friends. When I became Aircraft Commander a week or so before he did, he became my first co-pilot.

Then came a time later, as Aircraft Commander of his own aircraft, Charlie and I were in a very hot LZ. We were both taking hits. But one round hit his transmission while we were picking up South Vietnamese troops. He shut his engine down.

He and I were the last two ships in the LZ. Knowing without question to this very day decades later that he would not have left me sitting there, I waited for him.

Danielson, his crew and passengers left their disabled plane, raced across the sixty-feet of dry rice paddy and clambered aboard my ship.

Dangerously overloaded, we lurched along a good, seemed like a half mile of rice paddies, sometimes bouncing from dike to dike. We often took our only lift bouncing mid-skid on the concrete like dikes before we finally got airborne. Getting that unbelievably over-grossed airplane off the ground, gunships swooping down on both sides protecting us and encouraging me was my best flying ever. Still is.

Charlie bought the drinks that night. Those times and the camaraderie are gone. Charlie is gone too. Killed in a later mission near a mountain call Nui Ba Din.

All that is left now are the memories. And why should I bother with them? For all the pain and anguish they bring. For all the nights of little or no sleep – troubled if it comes at all – I would do well to forget! But I couldn't forget if I tried. All the faces weren't nameless. There will always be Mike Goeller, my Midwest, corn fed door gunner. Sometimes, driving alone late at night, unbidden, the memory of him slips in on me.

Mike was a farm boy, an excellent marksman, and the best doorgunner I ever had. He also became a very good friend. He was a big, broad-shouldered type, soft-spoken, easy-going, big-hearted and very open. I know for a fact none of his friends ran short of funds on their leaves or R&R's. Yet he never took one himself.

Truly his only serious shortcoming was a knack for getting his sandy colored hair cut as if the barber had placed a bowl on his head and snipped off any hair showing. This always made him look like a big, friendly giant. Or one of those trolls of Scandinavian folklore. Bigger though.

With a company policy of changing aircrews constantly, how Mike came to be my door-gunner is a story in itself. He had flown with me randomly on several occasions. After one particularly hairy mission, he said he would rather fly with me than any pilot in the company. Actually, what he said was, "He would fly straight into hell with me if we had to because he knew I'd fly him back out." I took this to be a pilot's supreme compliment and one I still cherish. Just a few days later, I had reason to return this compliment.

We were making a nine-ship troop insertion into a very, very hot LZ. We were the last ship in the flight and providing full suppression on the right – Mike's side as well as mine. Usually Aircraft Commanders took the left seat. I preferred the right seat in helicopters, the left seat when I fly fixed wing. Weird, but I also always take my sunglasses off on short final with either airplane. No explanation.

Since we were again, the last ship that day, I knew Mike would be watching and firing in the right rear quadrant of the aircraft. I had picked my spot to land. The dry rice paddy had a two-foot high dike about fifteen feet to the right of my touchdown point. With only a second to go before landing, we were moving slowly forward and settling rapidly to the ground.

In my peripheral vision I saw a figure in black pajamas pop up, chest high over the dike. This was not an accident. The tactic of hiding until the helicopter has landed right next to them was proven to be deadly effective. In that millisecond before touchdown, I turned to look at the figure and saw a Viet Cong soldier with an AK-47 automatic rifle pointed at my face. This was a common tactic of theirs. They would hide tightly beside a dike then pop up and ambush the aircraft when it was only a few feet away. My fear was so complete and intense, my mind completely blanked. I was incapable of even thinking the words, "Mike, cover me!"

But Mike had seen him...or her, calculated range and trajectory, and quickly swung that heavy M-60 machine gun forward and pulled off a quick lethal burst. All that in the time it takes to blink an eye and see your short, precious life pass in review.

That night, I bought a round of drinks in the enlisted men's club. Mike and I flew together always after that. We talked a great deal at makeshift airfields in the middle of nowhere, shut down after a flight, waiting for the call back to action. I learned about this big man's love for little children.

He could manage to find them, and they him, when we stopped near any village. He would always design some fascinating game that the children absolutely loved, right on the spot.

His intense love for kids did get out of hand though. Once he smuggled a small boy into the cubbyhole beside his door-gunner's seat. He knew we were going to a cold landing zone and coming right back, so he gave the kid his first and probably, his only helicopter ride. I just happened to look back as he was putting the child down after we landed back at the village. I was angry when I told Mike never to do anything like that again. But my heart was never really into scolding him.

I knew from our conversations that Mike had been drafted and hated the Army. He was just marking time, "playing the game," until he could get out and return to his family and land. He had a wife – only a bride, really. They had married only a couple of weeks before he left for Vietnam.

When Mike heard about his wife's pregnancy, he lost all semblance of order. He stopped total strangers to tell them about it. He bubbled over with happiness like the child he still was himself. He would physically stop an officer, address him with, "Hey, guess what?" and proceed to tell him about the expected arrival. Only the most hard-nosed, calloused, jerk-officer in the world would have reprimanded Mike for his breach of military discipline. To my knowledge, none did.

Mike had a plan. A plan born in a dream. When he got home, he would take his wife and baby, who would be about three months old by then, to a special place he had on a mountaintop near home. He would take a tent and food for a month and just get to know them. No guns. No noise. No people. Certainly, no helicopters. Just his wife, his baby and him, loving each other. Mike would be nineteen and a half by then. It was a beautiful dream.

With the baby's due date approaching, Mike tried to get special leave to go home while his wife had their child. He applied at Company level and was refused. So, he went over their heads and applied at Battalion level. Refused again. He offered to extend his tour of duty when he returned. Nothing. Door-gunners were desperately needed. Mike gave up. He resigned himself to meeting his child when they were both a little older.

One day, months later, all the 116th troop- carrying helicopters were down for maintenance. Our Stingers, a heavy gun team was tasked to go out in support of some ground troops working the "Iron Triangle" again. The gun team was short a door-gunner. Mike was asked to go.

He should have never flown with anybody but me.

The afternoon was dry, hot and windy. The gunships had run into real trouble only two miles from our base at Cu Chi. They were taking very heavy fire from an invisible enemy concealed in the dense foliage.

The gunship crew members were wearing the new "bullet-proof

helmets." These helmets were designed to withstand up to a .30 caliber bullet. So, the odds against what happened were incredible. But nevertheless, Mike took a hit, apparently in his forehead. Constructed to keep injury at bay, the helmet captured the bullet and held it inside, ricocheting around and around until its energy was spent. There was nothing recognizable left of Mike's head. When the ambulance met them at our airstrip I could see Mike's blood splattered all the way up to the gun ship's windscreen.

I was first stunned. Then hurt beyond anything I had ever felt in my life for the loss of this farm boy I had grown to love. But the pain had only just started.

Two days later a message arrived for Mike through the Red Cross. His wife had given birth to a healthy baby boy. I had filled the interim two days with grieving, drinking, some weeping, and lots of bad flying. This message very nearly shattered what little composure I had left.

I knew that the Red Cross message notifying Mike about his wife and baby would have taken about two days from the states. The messages had to pass each other in the mail and the two occurrences must have happened within a day of each other if not on the very same day.

To describe my feelings then is beyond words. Anger, frustration, pain and remorse are just empty collections of assorted letters. Compared to the abysmal loss I felt, language fails.

I felt a door shut behind me. The passage I was making from who I was, to who I would become, was clearly one way. There was no going back.

The Pan Am flight kept me traveling and visiting with people all over the world. Invited into homes, discussions, dinners, American movies with subtitles and catharsis. To a degree I purged some demons along the way. Nearly all I met wanted to know what was really going on in Vietnam. After two tours I still wasn't sure. It would be a couple decades before I was.

Iceland...

CRAP. NEAL, THE stringer, the war correspondent and devout cynic is coming down the aisle as we board in Heathrow for Iceland. Doesn't ask, just plops down in the empty seat next to me and says, "Hey, last leg Army. Finally going home?

"Almost. I'm getting off in Reykjavik for a while. Been learning my way around the world." I thought for a moment and said, "Hey, hope you're not headed for another conflict, like in America?"

"Nope, going to go home to Chicago and marry my girl. Going to go to work for the local paper and settle down, make babies–three she tells me–and write about politics. As if that will ever be interesting."

"You should be happy...excited. You don't sound enthusiastic about it."

"I'm not thrilled about day to day at a newspaper. This life of mine is an adrenaline rush and highly addictive. But if I don't stop my whirlwind tour of strife and grief the girl won't marry me. And I am enthusiastic about her."

"Sounds like she's a smart one," I offered. "I hope she makes you happy."

"We'll see. I hope it works out."

We're both quiet for a moment listening to an announcement from the cabin crew.

"You're wrong Neal. You know, about everything you told me before ... Life isn't about fighting. It's all about caring and hope."

"Hope? Well, maybe you're right. This woman is my hope. My last I think. I've been immersed in the world's killing and dying for ten years now. She's never even seen anyone die violently. Never watched another human hate so fiercely that they killed someone else ten feet away. I'm going to soak up her innocence, draw somehow from her purity and try to get back to whoever or whatever it was I used be. Like to see if I can still be who I was before I learned to reach for a camera instead of helping or trying to stop what's about to happen."

"Long journey to there and back. Hope it works out for you. I mean that."

I was wrong. About language, communicating. In Reykjavik I learned there are indeed language barriers. Icelandic has no root words you can identify. I don't think they even understand each other when you listen to their conversations. I think they're faking it, making up unintelligible noises and language as they go to impress the tourists. It's that unique. The surprise came when I found they were taught better English than I in their public schools.

The city of Reykjavik makes you feel like you haven't left Europe yet. Quaint, spotlessly clean, most of it old village style buildings like in Frankfurt and Brussels. Outside their only city is a land filled with geologic wonders. Geysers, streams hot enough to give off steam yet meandering through green grasslands.

It's also filled with a people truly misnamed "Icelanders" Their warmth as a people bubbles right up to the surface Like the lava in their volcanoes. They should all be wearing signs around their necks, "Welcome to our country...we know we've got a good thing going here."

Amazed to learn that women there have had equal rights in property and voting for nearly eight hundred years. The first parliament on the planet was formed there. No wonder everyone I met was so obviously proud of their country. Reminded me of a cabbie I met once in Italy. My next stop would be home.

Home…

THE OFFERED BROTHERHOOD gets you through the fighting.

The healing you do on your own.

Oddly, the coming home didn't work out too well. Today if someone finds out you were military they thank you for your service. Well intentioned and appreciated, of course. But the most powerful thing to say to a Vietnam vet is, "Welcome home." We didn't hear that for around our first three to four decades back.

I had missed two Christmases and two birthdays while I was away. All but the first birthday passed without notice. Just another day of flying. But the first birthday happened while I was in the 116th. My mom had baked a cake for me and sent it weeks in advance to be safe. Still the mail being what it was the cake arrived weeks after my birthday so, a couple months in the mail. When I opened it, it was rock hard, actually a chocolate brick. The pilots in my platoon always shared whatever food sent us from home, cookies, brownies - whatever. So, I shared.

It went something like this... We would literally hatchet off a chunk of chocolate brick. We would put it on a metal plate-tray from the mess hall then soak it in either Schlitz or Blatz beer to soften it up. Hard to express the yummy factor. Surprised the ice cream manufacturers haven't by now tried to duplicate this truly arresting flavor. Thanks mom.

I had seen combat and the world. I can't quantify the reparations I realized through Pan Am Flight One. I am certain that had I gone straight home with all the baggage and horror of war fresh in my mind and heart I would be the lesser for it.

I would have started my life over in America, still the monster. Meeting people all around the planet, being embraced by them, welcomed back to a caring, giving tribe had somehow begun to restore my faith in humanity. I had regained some hope for us all. It was cathartic, therapeutic, healthy. Not sure yet it was enough.

Fears don't leave just because you leave Vietnam or any other theater of war I suspect. They take a while to go away. Some never do.

Vietnam was like being kept in a totally dark room – no windows, no doors, no light anywhere. I had been in a state of terror and exhaustion for a year and a half. Suddenly, one October morning I was sent home. I stepped back into brilliant sunshine and complete personal freedom. Mind and body intact. The mornings after I came home were decidedly different from Vietnam's black uncertainty.

Once stateside, certainty returned to focus, and it was followed instantly by undiluted joy and elation. I wanted to exercise my mind. I wanted to learn all I could, read everything. I wanted to talk with the intellectuals, tell them what I knew of the world, of people. And mostly, of the awesome things I had learned about myself.

I wanted to run faster and jump higher than any human ever had. I wanted to throw myself down soft green hills, roll to the bottom, land on my feet and run forever as I did as a child. I felt I could play every instrument in the orchestra like a virtuoso and win every athletic event I could enter. Yes, I wanted to show off a little. Not for a crowd or the girl next door. For me. For being alive!

Now, when I think of those who would never come home, I feel selfish for reveling in my good fortune. But that didn't quash my spirits then. I had made it! I was alive. And that had never meant so much before.

There were other emotions, feelings and sensations to deal with though. All part of my "psychological adjustment" to peacetime civilian life. Sometimes I felt revulsion at what I had seen and taken part in. Guilt over willingly going to a war that I then didn't understand disturbed me a lot at times. I could not rationalize my guilt away. Eventually though, I have come to believe, I was far less culpable than the elected officials responsible for that travesty. Yet, this is next to no consolation at all. It still bothers me.

I was often deeply troubled by and again, felt surprisingly guilty, over the lottery of fate that decides I should live and others should die. What serendipitous force determined that a man sitting next to me in the cockpit of an aircraft, with a wife and three children at home should die and I should not? If there is reason and logic, not just names pulled out of some celestial hat, behind "that" force I hope I fulfill whatever purpose it is that made my survival possible.

I've been back from Vietnam for forty-seven years. In the beginning, fears, rather than memories, were my strongest and most frequent sensation. Fears come in all sizes. Some are large and can fill me nearly to overflowing. If not kept under control, these large sudden fears manifest themselves as panic or shock.

A fear of this size consumed me for an instant on an early, quiet Los Angeles morning. Having had experienced a few weeks of peace after returning from Vietnam, unneeded defenses were slowly being worn down. Suddenly, there was an explosion and for a split second I was reliving the terror of my first nighttime rocket attack at Cu Chi.

I was relieved to discover that Los Angeles was experiencing a major earthquake.

There are also small, gnawing fears. These fears must periodically be dealt with or somehow suppressed. One fear I still get, though less now as I grow older, is having to go back to another war somewhere. With all the technical flight training I received, I had been told that I would be called before an untrained man off the street. Officers are always Active or Inactive Reserve, never discharged. Age has its rewards after all. Long since passed the time. They won't take me now.

Sometimes these fears and memories trigger larger, more terrible concerns. I worry that this nation's leaders, willingly, for suspect motives, expended 58,715 American lives and untold thousands of Vietnamese lives on a stalling action. They knowingly merely postponed what those in power knew to be inevitable.

The fear of personally going back to war lessens with age. But, the concern and the shame I have for our buck-passers and flesh-pressers, simply grows with perspective and time. This claim is not unfounded.

Thanks to a fluke, common enough in the military, I spent the last month of my first tour and all my second tour of Vietnam as a VIP pilot. I flew for two Generals. The first was General Walter Richardson, the then Military Governor of Saigon, responsible directly to and only to President Nixon. Richardson was a wonderful mad man who loved to fly low and fast, leaning out the open side of the ship, allowing the wind to blast through his sparse, white hair.

When Richardson left Vietnam, I wanted to go back to the Hornets, the 116th Assault. Vern Estes was the detachment commander for the five VIP pilots and two crews and barely a friend then. But strangely, over the last forty some years he has proven to be one of my best.

Vern spent three days trying to convince me that I'd made it out of combat and didn't need to go back. Despite that offering of brotherhood in combat, if they had the chance to get out too, they would. I didn't owe them.

General Richardson however, had already called General Creighton Abrams, the Four-Star Military Theater Commander, Vietnam. General Abrams oversaw all troops, all action, all allied forces And all other Generals. Gen Richardson simply told him I should be his new pilot.

Two days later I took over as Aircraft Commander on the highest profile mission for the highest- ranking officer in the theater. As such I was privy to some treasured but brief conversations. General Abrams was quite a man and a great General.

His career had gotten an early boost while he was a young Colonel commanding a tank battalion during the Battle of the Bulge, WWII. I admired him. He and his wife were very good to me for years after I left the Army. Abrams wrote letters that helped me get into law school.

HEADQUARTERS
UNITED STATES MILITARY ASSISTANCE COMMAND, VIETNAM
OFFICE OF THE COMMANDER
APO SAN FRANCISCO 96222

MACJOO   1 October 1970

CW2 Richard W. Jellerson,
Saigon VIP Detachment
120th Assault Helicopter Company
APO 96307

1. On your departure from Vietnam and separation from the United
States Army, I wish to extend my personal appreciation for your
service as Aircraft Commander and Pilot of my command and control
helicopter.

2. Throughout your assignment to Headquarters, United States
Military Assistance Command, Vietnam, I have been impressed by
your professional attitude, technical skill, experience, and dedication. The standard of performance you set exemplifies the high
quality of our country's young men who have willingly carried more
than their share of the load in Vietnam.

3. I congratulate you on your accomplishments while in the United
States Army and wish you continued success in the future.

CREIGHTON W. ABRAMS
General, United States Army
Commanding

As I left the Army, General Abrams wrote this wonderful letter

Yes, an 8 by 10 glossy of Abe autographed to me

One of the most common missions I flew for "Abe" was that of picking him up at headquarters and dropping him onto the roof heliport of the U.S. Embassy in downtown Saigon. There he would meet with Ambassador Bunker for hours. I would shut the ship down and wait for him.

Ultimately, his Aide de Camp, then a Colonel Noel, would radio, "Crank it up!" We'd start the ship. Abe would appear top of the stairs, walk to the aircraft and plug into the intercom. Every time before he or the aid would tell me where we needed to go next the General would plug in and say, "God damn politicians got my hands tied."

A direct quote. Every time.

Heard that indictment in my sleep for a couple years after leaving the Army. While it was only an unsettling indictment then, in hindsight, it is awesome and terrifying.

Like General Westmoreland before him, he had a plan to end and win that ugly war. But he was only a military man. The course of this painful American episode would be decided by our trustworthy elected officials.

Interesting story involving Colonel Noel. Mornings he would call me to discuss our missions that day. If we were to fly that day, he would tell me we are taking Abe to the Embassy or wherever else he wanted to go. One day he called about flying the General to the embassy, but the local winds were such I told him we couldn't fly the rooftop pad. Strong winds burbling over the roof edge ten floors up could be hazardous. His cool response, "Okay, we'll drive." But the Major then commanding the 120th Aviation Company heard about me refusing to fly the General's mission.

Smug and cocky as General Abrams' Aircraft Commander.

Our two birds and crews were attached to the 120th for maintenance and payroll. The Major flew down and got me into the little waiting lounge we built, "locked my heels" (had me come to attention) while he berated me for refusing to fly General Abrams. He said, "Your job is to fly the General." My response directly back into his face only inches from mine, "Actually sir, my job is to fly the General...safely!"

The next day Colonel Noel locked that Major's heels right in front of me, again in our lounge. He lashed into him telling him, "Don't ever tell Mr. Jellerson how or when to fly. General Abrams likes how he flies." There was more. Later, Vern told me that a superior officer is never supposed to dress down a lower grade officer in front of anyone with an even lower rank. The entire show was for my benefit.

I also learned that junior officers are never supposed to prank senior officers, especially Generals. But it happens. Our detachment of five pilots for the two Four Star Generals' two helicopters had a fixed-wing and crew equivalent across the base. The fixed-wing flight crew had a beautiful twin engine Beechcraft at their disposal. This aircraft was used for longer in-country flights out of range for our Hueys. We knew the other pilots of course. When time permitted we gave each other stick time as all of us wanted to be dual rated. I forget which General they were flying one day but well into one flight things took a strange turn.

The night before, the pilot and co-pilot had gone to the officer's club and filled a paper bag with empty beer cans. At 15,000 feet the General was in back reading a report. There was a partition between the pilots' seats and the cabin and suddenly, an empty beer can rolled and clanked down the aisle toward the general. A moment later the pilots released another empty on a journey down the aisle to the General. I'm told it took four or five empties before the General even reacted.

Calmly, knowing he was being pranked, he paid them back in a most civil but never-the-less painful way. He went forward to the cockpit, returned their empties and without even acknowledging the prank or scolding them gave them a new destination. Mid-flight, this is not easy. It requires a total reconfiguring of the instrument flight course. As they finished the new course and artillery clearances requiring several new calculations and radio calls, they promptly informed their passenger. The General promptly then continued changing the destination again and again and again. At one point, suggesting they just put down at An Loc for ice cream. But whatever it takes to lighten up your day in war.

Flying General Abrams was an honor and quite the education for a twenty-year old. Vern told me years later that I was the most natural pilot he had ever flown with. As he went on to fly professionally until his retirement I consider this another cherished compliment.

Myself, Don Curtis and Paul Mac Michaels, all General's pilots

Back home I learned there are even smaller, but no less demanding fears. Some take a great deal of time to show up. Sometimes we live with fears, adjusting to them without realizing what they are. I discovered this for myself not long ago.

Several years after Vietnam, I looked for an old friend from Army Flight School. I have been in his town. I found his last name listed in the phone book. Only four entries. I didn't call. I have been to the small airport where he used to work and failed to ask if anyone there knew him.

After a year of intense flight training and fun, Ron and I lost track of one another in Vietnam. Since I heard he had drawn decent duty, his chances of returning home were very good. Upon leaving Vietnam, however, I ran into another classmate who said that we lost over forty percent of our Flight School graduating class either wounded in combat and sent home or Killed in Action.

Maybe Ron wasn't one of these.

I don't know. I never will know.

Ron had raised loving life to an art form. He was gregarious, nearly bohemian in lifestyle. He had studied acting before getting into the Army and seemed to have the right quip or quote for any occasion, complete with appropriate histrionics. He was brighter than most of our instructors and delighted in helping them illustrate that fact.

It was his idea, the time as Officer Candidates that the entire company showed up at morning formation with our bright orange Solo Flight badges buttoned over the wrong pocket. In flight school these were given out only after you had soloed in a helicopter. This gross deviation from dress uniform would have gone unnoticed despite our fifty barely suppressed smiles, had it not been for one late arrival who had not heard the word. Naturally, this odd ball made us stick out like fifty sore thumbs. Still, we enjoyed the prank and camaraderie even throughout the punishing push-ups. Later, the mere mention of the training officer's expression as he saw through our little plot sent us into spasms of hysterical laughter.

Ron made military life bearable and military discipline laughable, often the butt of much well-timed humor. He was fun loving, and life was precious to him. That's how I remember him. And I'm going to always imagine him living life to the fullest. I dropped any pretense of my search long ago. I know this is a form of denial. But I'd rather believe him to be alive yet never see him again, than to discover his beautiful life was wasted in that stupid goddamn war.

Strangely, that war sometimes seems like it happened just yesterday. I will, sometimes, find myself writing of it in the present tense.

Flying through Agent Orange daily in 1969 resulted in my acquiring lymphatic cancer in 1995. My family was in medicine but encouraged me to go to the Veterans Administration Hospital. I did, and I beat it.

Dr. David Wilbur was the VA head Oncologist and over the last twenty years of checkups became a friend. He reminded me once of my reaction to his diagnosis of cancer. I said, "Doctor, you're late, I've already handled this. I'm over it. Do what you have to do."

David says, "Well let's schedule you for chemo."

My response, "Schedule me hell. I'm here right now, let's get after it." He told me later I beat cancer with my attitude. "Nice I let the medical community's therapies come along for the ride," he added.

When I go to the VA hospital for checkups though and see a guy my age in a wheelchair with no legs I wonder. Just in my own quiet, private hell, I wonder if it's one of the guys I picked up over there.

Can't know. Beyond that first medevac I never saw who we were picking up. We were under fire and they needed medical attention as fast as possible. Fly the mission and get them to the hospital pad as fast as you can. You don't check IDs, you just know they are wounded.

At the med-evac pad they are taken off the airplane by hurried, dedicated medics. You don't ever know if they had only lost a leg or bled to death on the way. And I don't want to know now.

Whether you think you need it or not, approval or validation of your efforts in any endeavor can be important. It sometimes comes in strange ways. Questions still exist about our purpose, goals and accomplishments in Vietnam. If the war remains veiled in a fog for the American public those of us who went and fought are resolute we did everything right.

I was doing a film for The History Channel titled "Personal Experience, Helicopter Warfare in Vietnam." Easiest and at once, the toughest film I have ever done. I was with my film crew at Fort Rucker, Alabama. Film crews pride themselves on wearing really ratty clothes. It's like a daily competition among them. Holes in their jeans and truly well-worn T-shirts are de rigueur. I was dressed comfortably, with long hair, a beard and flip flops. Not directly competing with the guys but, you get the idea.

My crew was crawling all over a very cool multi-million dollar Apache Helicopter getting shots of everything we were allowed as the training battalion commander walked up. Captain Saul was frosty, I felt definite icing conditions. He had been ordered to help me with the film and reluctantly, he would.

As he asked how he could help, his back was to the final approach of the training field behind him. I noticed over his shoulder an Apache on short final. It was stair-stepping, an unsteady hobby horse flight rather than the normal steady straight line with constant slowing to touch down. I told him it looked like a bird was in trouble behind him. He turned looked and said, "No, he's just under the bag" meaning he was on instruments. The captain then said, "How did you know he was in trouble?"

I said, "Well, I trained here myself few years back". And it was suddenly like he wanted to start over. As he straightened himself, it looked like he might even reintroduce himself. "Vietnam?" he asked. "Yeah, two tours. Hueys." I replied. Then he asked, "Mr. Jellerson, how can I help you?" "Well I'd love to film the Apache at work on the firing range, but the Public Affairs Officer said I can't."

"Really?" he said. "Can your guys be at the range around two today? "Yes, they can." "Give me a minute." And he walked over to the Colonel P. A. O. who outranked him and said, "I just invited Mr. Jellerson and his film crew to the firing range this afternoon...I'll bet you have a lot of phone calls to make, sir."

That afternoon we set up on the helipad next to his Apache's pad. He pulled the aircraft up to a forty-foot hover and started firing. The brass from the fifty caliber rounds tinkled down from his aircraft so close we could hear them landing randomly on the concrete pad. Then he fired off two of his Hellfire missiles. Awesome.

But then, the most amazing thing...he cocked the aircraft at about a 45-degree angle and gave the controls to his student in the front seat. From that cockpit he looked down and gave me a snappy salute. As a validation of my service, that was the most important salute I'll ever have. I hope Captain Saul survived his service.

The next validation by another warrior came more subtly. I was doing another documentary film titled "A Solemn Promise, America's Missing in Action." Our nation has over 82,000 MIAs. Incredible in itself. The other powerful story element is that, proudly, our country never stops looking for them, ever. Through some help from Department of Defense I had learned of a yearly reunion of the survivors of the Battle of Kham Duc. I knew in the early stages of the film everyone would understand how when a plane goes missing or a Navy vessel does not come back from a mission, there are obvious MIAs. But how in hand-to-hand combat, face to face with the enemy could there be any infantry MIAs?

Kham Duc was the most horrific engagement of the Vietnam War. It lasted only two days but with hundreds killed on both sides and 31 of ours Missing in Action. Bill Wright was awarded the Silver Star for his heroism at that battle. I had just met Bill and we were having dinner in an excellent hotel in Oklahoma. I was having my usual aged, single malt scotch with dinner and Bill and I were talking easily.

We were just getting to know each other when a second scotch appeared. The waiter said it came from, "Those gentlemen at the bar." At the bar there were three guys my age. Bill said they were also with the reunion. I waved my thanks but kept my seat. Soon two more scotches showed up for me. I hadn't even finished my first. So, I excused myself and went to the bar.

One of the guys said, "I know you're here to film Bill, but he tells me you were an Army helicopter pilot". I said, "Yes I was, but why the drinks?' The vocal one says, "Because you were a helicopter pilot in Viet Nam." "Well yeah I was, but not at your battle," I replied. The vocal one goes on, "Doesn't matter. For what you guys did over there for us on the ground there's never going to be an Army pilot within a hundred miles of me that will ever buy his own drinks. Thank you."

It was another rewarding validation and a kind of flash back to that incredible bond we shared in combat. I'm proud to be a part of it but membership in that club has a price.

I've accomplished a lot since that war. I've done well and done badly too, and grown through the pain. I've many times declared myself healed. I know I mostly am healed, healthy, and happy. That war shouldn't be a problem or even much of an issue at this late date.

So, how is it that a simple human gesture could bring me to my emotional knees?

My youngest brother was getting married at an elegant and sweet little ceremony in the backyard of a friend's home. It was warm and sunny. Southern California was doing its best for all of us. The old ritual complete, there were cousins and aunts galore to mingle with. It was fun. Just about the last to leave, I saw one of my cousins moving right toward me. Craig is the usually jovial, good humored one. But he looked different somehow. He stopped in front of me and held out his hand to shake mine, then held it. I could feel he needed to say something important.

Maybe even tough or uncomfortable for him.

He simply said, "I don't know if anyone ever told you this. Maybe no one ever said it before. I just wanted to thank you for what you did in Viet Nam. I appreciate what you did and what it must have cost you. I'm sorry I never said it before. Thank you."

If I'm truly healed, and it's really all behind me, it should have been really easy to just say something easy and flip like, "Thanks Craig. That was nice." I probably did as a defense mechanism.

I don't know for sure what I said. I do know it took all the strength I could muster to get to my car before I started crying. It wasn't just a manly little weep. It was decades of pent up pain, frustration, fears and remorse at my loss of innocence, my loss of trust in our system, my loss of friends I should still have and my own gullibility.

And, I think, probably much more I still don't comprehend.

No one had ever thanked me before. I didn't believe I needed it. I couldn't either believe that the simple gesture could pull me back down so far so quickly. Obviously, it is not something I've left too far behind. But I don't want to wear that war with my heart on my shirtsleeve.

It's funny what we think we need and don't need. Animals are so good at determining exactly what they need. They seldom ever try to get more than they need, or anything they don't need at all. The human race however, self-proclaimed superiors of these lowly beasts, has pornography, drugs, alcohol, unhealthy relationships with one another, wars, child abuse, and more. You'd think, with intellect, our only pure separation from the rest of the animals, we would be better at determining our "needs." I certainly wish I could. We're a strange lot.

I'm back in Southern California. I still love burgers, football, the beach and girls. I call them women now. My friends tell me there's still a lot of little boy left in me. This is okay. I'm surprised though. I think they mean I still have a sense of curiosity about how and why human nature works. I can still be surprised…and disappointed.

I'm still amazed at what we fight over. It's always property or ideologies. We should fight against poverty, illiteracy or disease as hard. It seems the human sentiment strong enough to start wars is, "I'm right – you're wrong!" or "That's mine!" I'm not qualified to preach, just observe, as a man who experienced a war. And my observations lead me to believe we should be better than that as a species. Above it.

But if we can't stop wars, I know, without question, we shouldn't send teenagers to fight them. Teenagers should be left home to discover life, sports, and rediscover sex every weekend. True love every month. They shouldn't be catapulted unprepared through a baptism of fire and blood then bungee-corded back to America. Unprepared again. And so many don't even come home.

Children...born, fed, reared, loved, educated, cared for by parents and loved ones for eighteen years then killed by political imperative. This is the only lasting essence of any war, in any country, in any culture at any time.

When I got back I was twenty-one years old. Yet I had aged spiritually too much to fit in. I know I returned world weary, out of step with my peers, too old for my age. The things I had learned and experienced had no real application in normal life. Two and a half years of credits that didn't apply toward graduation. Looking much like a fugitive, I've dodged nearly all of society's conventions and institutions.

Most of my friends married late in college. To their individual joy and torment, they have produced children. Their children's children are older now than I was when I went to Viet Nam. I see them, and I can't believe anyone could send an eighteen-year-old to war.

They're smarter, better educated today. But somehow more fragile, even less sure of themselves than we were. While they probably need not worry about a nuclear holocaust, we've given them lesser but so many more uncertainties to grow up with. I still have no children and have never married.

My core of early friends all have careers they have diligently and energetically pursued to varying degrees of success. I have as eagerly jumped from position to position, new challenge to new challenge. Usually I have been my own boss. Apparently, I'm unwilling to leave my fate to the decisions of others. This, a scary lesson I know I learned in Vietnam.

I have been a long-haul truck driver, copywriter, law student, account executive for advertising agencies, principal of my own agency, salesman, marketing consultant, businessman, photographer, concert promoter, personal manager in the music industry, sales trainer, documentary filmmaker and writer. I've traveled extensively including a few trips around the world and visited some special countries several times.

Outwardly I must appear to be just outside the norm. To some, I'm sure I appear dysfunctional. I have taken way too many chances in my business life. Not enough in my personal life. Sometimes I feel I've missed something. I know I've missed some things but gained much as well.

I don't know if things would have worked out differently if I hadn't gone to Vietnam. I'll never know. I didn't really expect to sustain that adrenaline rush longer than the year and a half it lasted anyway.

So, I'm healed. All better now.

But it's the 4th of July and I just left a wonderful party with good friends across the lake where I live. Left before the fireworks started. I hate fireworks. Love my country but hate the 4th of July.

The celebration instantly takes me back to a specific horrifying mission.

I was flying an empty slick behind our gunship lead for a prisoner pick up. Infantry we dropped a few minutes ago had captured enemy soldiers and they would need to be interrogated. I was about a hundred feet behind the lead gunship doing at least a hundred miles an hour three to four feet off the deck.

The lead gunship instantly took heavy fire from a tree line on his left. The pilot on the controls must have been hit and he flew the ship directly into the ground. As I said, downed Huey's all blow up three times. I banked hard right but flew through the first explosion: fuel. Yellow flames, black smoke instantly on impact. Banked around hard again to the left to circle and see if there were survivors. The two remaining gunships escorting me on my right and left circled too, a little higher. They couldn't stop to help, too heavy to land but flew cover for me. I could stop and land for survivors if there were any.

The second explosion was magnesium parts of the transmission burning white hot. Looked very much like our own white phosphorus missiles exploding. The third explosion is ammunition, rounds cooking off. As a gunship it was armed with an amazing collection of mortars, rockets, grenades and machine gun ammunition.

Next time you see a firework display you'll see and hear what I saw that day. Random, arbitrary explosions of different sizes and projectiles of different breathtaking colors. Until the cook off I circled close enough to feel the heat. No survivors.

Amazing I had to leave the 4th of July party early but still feel I'm healthy and well. Obviously, the healing continues.

After a career in advertising and marketing I turned to documentary films. I wrote and produced a documentary for The History Channel titled "Personal Experience, Helicopter Warfare in Vietnam" Proud of that one. But, as I said, it was both the toughest and easiest film I ever did. Too close to it. I've done films about other subjects. Close friends and family suggest though I gravitate toward military issues. Maybe I'm a voice for those issues. One of them anyway.

I recently finished producing a film titled "A Solemn Promise, America's Missing in Action" about our MIA service members still unaccounted for. As of this writing; that number stands at 82,348 since World War II. Wars demand a great deal of healing. I came home via sixteen other countries to begin my healing. And I'm apparently still a work in progress. But these Americans are still missing-still out there somewhere waiting to be found. Their families, as you can well imagine, can't heal either for a lack of closure. Proudly, we, as a nation, promise we never leave anyone behind. America has promised its citizens and is committed to never stop searching for these still missing fallen warriors.

The arm of the government responsible for these searches is the Defense POW/MIA Accounting Agency (DPAA). As a bureaucracy it is often mired down in excessive paperwork and political roadblocks while dealing with the many countries around the world where these often-hazardous searches must take place. Still their teams work 24/7 to help keep the promise made by our country to those of us our country puts in harm's way. Perhaps we can all heal, find solace and a substantial deserved pride in this honorable search for our MIAs. That is my heartfelt hope.

I'm a positive person and optimistic about the future. The only dream

I know I can't fulfill is being happily married to my high school sweetheart for the last forty-five years. Other than that, looking back, about all I missed was a slow, happy, safe transition from childhood to manhood.

"The Healing, Pan American Flight 001"
© 2018 R Jellerson, Storyteller Press
WGAw registered   All rights reserved

NEIL A. ARMSTRONG
P.O. BOX 436
LEBANON, OH 45036

May 24, 2001

Mr. Richard Jellerson
P. O. Box 389
Seal Beach, CA 90740

Dear Mr. Jellerson:

Thank you for your letter and essay relating to our intersection in Viet Nam.

You were among the many who were putting yourselves in harm's way at the time. I could appreciate it more than most, having done the same 2 decades earlier. I just wanted to thank you and testify that there would be a life awaiting you.

All the best.

Sincerely,

Neil A. Armstrong

NAA:vw

Neil Armstrong read an early draft of chapter one.

Richard Jellerson
richard@storytellerfilms.tv
Screen our films at ...storytellerfilms.tv
Storyteller Press is a DBA of Storyteller Original Films LLC

CPSIA information can be obtained
at www.ICGtesting.com
Printed in the USA
FSHW01n2222160918
52321FS